From Reading to Writing

John W. Presley
William Dodd

Augusta College

Holt, Rinehart and Winston
New York   Chicago   San Francisco   Atlanta   Dallas
Montreal   Toronto

Library of Congress Cataloging in Publication Data
Main entry under title:

Breakthrough, from reading to writing.

1. College readers.   2. English language—Rhetoric.
I. Presley, John W.   II. Dodd, William, date.
PE1417.B687   808'.04275   79–20526

ISBN 0–03–048766–8

Acknowledgments

"Everybody Knows Benny Capalbo Invented the Grinder" by W. G. Nicholson. Reprinted with permission from the October 1976 issue of *Yankee Magazine* published by Yankee, Inc., Dublin, NH.

"Violinist Isaac Stern Is a Unique Virtuoso" by Joseph Roddy. Reprinted with permission from the January 31, 1977 issue of *People Weekly,* text by Joseph Roddy © Time Inc.

"Strivers' Row" and "Mollie Moon" by Stephen Birmingham, from *Certain People* by Stephen Birmingham. Copyright © 1977 by Stephen Birmingham. By permission of Little, Brown and Co.

"James Dickey's Glory" by James Dickey, from *Esquire* (October, 1976) Reprinted by permission of *Esquire* magazine; © 1976 by Esquire, Inc.

From "Building Men the Marine Corps Way" by Harry Crews. Copyright © 1976 by Harry Crews. Originally appeared in *Esquire* Magazine. Reprinted by permission of Paul R. Reynolds, Inc., 599 Fifth Avenue, New York, NY 10017.

"Twenty-six Hours of Insanity: A Marijuana Nightmare" by Robert Tucker. Copyright © 1977 by the NYM Corporation. Reprinted with the permission of *New York* Magazine.

"Battle Scene" by John Steinbeck from *The Portable Steinbeck.* Copyright © 1971 by The Viking Press, Inc. Reprinted by permission of Viking Penguin Inc.

Excerpts from pp. 11–12 "July 1, 1776" in *The Birth of the United States* by Jim Bishop. Copyright © 1976 by Jim Bishop. By permission of William Morrow & Company.

From *Power! How to Get It, How to Use It* by Michael Korda. Copyright © 1975 by Michael Korda and Paul Gitlin, Trustee for the benefit of Christopher Korda. Reprinted by permission of Random House, Inc.

"The Spring, The Garden, The Outbuildings" by James Agee. From *Let Us Now Praise Famous Men* by James Agee. Copyright © renewed 1969 by Mia Fritsch Agee. Reprinted by permission of Houghton Mifflin Company.

Exerpts from *The Indian Heritage of America* by Alvin M. Josephy, Jr. Copyright © 1968 by Alvin M. Josephy, Jr. By permission of Bantam Books, Inc. All rights reserved.

To the Instructor

This book and the materials in it have been thoroughly tested in the classroom; the book has grown out of our efforts to give our basic writing students reading material to use as models for writing and to use as starting points for classroom discussions before writing. Both of us are English instructors, and both of us have also taught classes in reading. We have constantly looked for stimulating, college-level reading material for both composition and reading classes, and we have looked for a way of teaching both the meaning of essays for students whose reading level may not yet be equal to a particular essay and the structure of essays for students who need models for their own writing.

Our basic premise is this: If properly directed, good readers will become good writers.

To help a student become a good reader, we have provided exercises and writing-oriented activities that give vocabulary and comprehension practice.

To help a student become a good writer, we have provided exercises designed to lead the student to discover and imitate the organization of paragraphs and essays.

Our belief that good readers become good writers has led us to use an integrated approach to teaching students the correlated skills of reading and writing. We lead students to an understanding of basic organizational patterns by allowing them to observe these patterns in samples of both student and professional writing—both formal and informal—and by giving them the opportunity to apply these principles in their own writing.

The first chapter of the text treats the development of paragraphs with specific detail; Chapters 2, 3, and 4 introduce the student to narrative, descriptive, and comparison-contrast organization. Chapter 5 introduces the basic structure of the essay by emphasizing the similarities between essay organization and paragraph organization. These three patterns of organization are at once the simplest and most useful for students to master, and they are the patterns most often taught in basic writing courses.

Each chapter has a short introductory section that uses student writing to introduce organization patterns, together with exercises that reinforce and develop the student's mastery of these patterns. These introductory sections are followed in each chapter by professional writing, which the student can analyze and imitate.

For each essay, one or two central and representative paragraphs are first selected and presented to the student as a shorter reading, with vocabulary items and questions about structure that lead to a close reading and understanding of these sample sections of the essay. Then when the student is presented with the entire essay, he or she will be better prepared to understand both the literal meaning of the essay and the structure and sequence of the paragraphs within it. Each entire essay is followed by further vocabulary questions, by questions about the structure of the essay, and by comprehension questions. This text makes certain that students can read and understand material before they attempt to analyze or imitate it.

Students using this text will find that a great deal of work and very close reading are demanded of them. Students should be encouraged to read slowly, to underline topic sentences and major ideas, to number sentences, to consult dictionaries—in short, to develop all of the habits that a good reader uses while reading academic texts. The many questions use repetition as a key learning device, as assurance that the student is faced with small increments of difficulty and with the maximum chance for success in answering each question.

Many English composition teachers find themselves urged or required, even if by circumstance only, to teach reading skills; so reading skills have been incorporated into each chapter.

As much as possible, answering the reading comprehension tests requires the same skills as are developed by the questions about structure. The comprehension tests cover a wide range of skills, including

1. Recalling facts (to complement discussions of paragraph development).

2. Locating facts (to complement discussions of rhetorical arrangement).

3. Sequencing details (to complement discussions of transitions).

4. Finding the main idea (to complement discussions of topic sentences).

5. Drawing conclusions (to complement discussions of concluding sentences).

6. Making inferences.

7. Paraphrasing.

8. Judging attitude and tone.

Many of the comprehension questions require the student to write a short paragraph in response.

In addition, the text concentrates on word attack skills, specifically developing the use of context clues. In each selection by a professional writer, words that are essential to a complete understanding of the passage have been underlined; in the next exercise, students are asked to write or choose text-specific definitions for these words. The vocabulary words have also been chosen and arranged so that the instructor may work beyond the scope of the exercise itself and deal with such skills as structural analysis and the identification of variant word meanings.

An *Instructor's Manual* is available. It may be obtained through a local Holt representative or by writing to the English Editor, Holt, Rinehart and Winston, 383 Madison Avenue, New York, NY 10017.

We wish to thank the following reviewers: Richard S. Beal; James S. Hill, Oklahoma State University, Stillwater; Lee Kolzow, William Rainey Harper College; James Peck, Jefferson State Junior College; and Nancy V. Wood, University of Texas, El Paso.

J. W. P.
W. D.

Augusta, Georgia

Contents

2 Chronological Arrangement of Detail 48

3 Description: Spatial Arrangement of Detail 106

4 Comparison-Contrast Arrangement of Detail   164

5 The Organization of Essays
220

Developing Paragraphs with Relevant Detail

1

Learning to write paragraphs or to read them depends upon your recognizing some facts about the structure of paragraphs. There are many different types, which you will learn about later, but all paragraphs have at least three characteristics in common.

1. *A paragraph is a group of sentences all about one topic.* Every sentence in any paragraph must be about the topic of that paragraph. A writer cannot "wander" off his topic. If he is ready to begin writing about another subject, the writer must indent and begin a new paragraph.[1]

2. *A paragraph develops or illustrates its topic by including specific details or examples, which help explain what the writer is saying.*

3. *A paragraph is planned.* All paragraphs have some sort of arrangement of their supporting details; the writer doesn't "go in circles" or repeat himself needlessly.

When readers approach any written material, they can automatically assume two things. First, writers have a purpose, or reason, for wishing to pass on the information they write down. Second, the material read is composed of an author's ideas, organized in some way and written down. Now, if a reader is to make sense of a written passage, the writer must organize his material into paragraphs. This alone is not enough. Within each paragraph the writer must also decide which thought will

[1]The use of the generic *he* is idiomatic in English and is not to be regarded as sexist.

come first, second, third, or last. To organize his paragraph, the writer usually begins with a *generalization*. This generalization is usually a thought that is broad enough in scope to contain the other *specific* thoughts in the paragraph. In this way, the writer provides a structure to guide the reader.

Exercises

1 Which of the following items is broad enough to be the *generalization* and contains all of the other items?

(Circle the correct answer.)

A. nails   D. wood

B. boards   E. carpentry

C. hammer   F. saw

2 In the following group, which item could serve as the *generalization*?

(Circle the correct answer.)

A. painting   C. poetry   E. music

B. art   D. fiction   F. sculpture

3 In the following group of phrases, which phrase could serve as the *generalization*?

(Circle the correct answer.)

A. Using the car more often.   D. Having a new sense of freedom.

B. Being better trusted by family.

C. Not having to bother parents for transportation.   E. Not having to ask other people's parents for transportation.

F. Going places alone.

4 In many paragraphs, the generalization will be contained in the first sentence, followed by the sentences that contain specific details. Put the following jumbled paragraph into order by placing numbers in the blanks.

_____   I can now use the car more often, without my parents' going along.

2

_____   I feel more trusted by my parents and friends.

_____   Receiving my driver's license was very important to me because it gave me a new sense of freedom.

_____   In addition, I no longer have to worry my father or other people about driving me somewhere when they don't want to go.

5 Read the following paragraph, and pick out the sentence which seems to state the paragraph's topic.

Some dogs are not suitable to be kept as pets in apartments. Beagles, for example, are hunting dogs and are famous for their loud barks and howls. Other dogs, such as setters or spaniels, need constant exercise, a problem for people who are not at home a great deal. Most importantly, some dogs, such as shepherds or St. Bernards, are simply too big to be kept in a small area.

1 What is the topic of the paragraph?

_____

The sentence in which the topic is stated is called the *topic sentence.* By "announcing" the subject, the topic sentence helps to control the paragraph by insuring that the paragraph is all about only the one subject announced and helps the reader by establishing immediately what the topic of the paragraph is and how the writer feels about it. Nearly all paragraphs have topic sentences; when a topic sentence is present, it is usually the first sentence, but it may sometimes be the middle or last sentence. The topic sentence, though, is always the one that contains the topic word, the word that is the subject of the paragraph.

2 Which sentences include the details or examples?

_____

_____

_____

These are called *support sentences,* and every paragraph has to be made up of support sentences, whether or not it has a topic sentence.

3 What three phrases introduce each different support sentence?

_____, _____, _____. These are examples of *transitions,* which a writer uses to help the reader understand the relationship between the support sentences. For example, by looking at the last transition used above, you should be able to tell why the sentence about shepherds and St. Bernards is given last.

6 Read the following paragraph carefully, paying close attention to the subject of the paragraph and to its development with supporting detail.

My neighborhood is large, quiet, and friendly. My neighborhood is so large that I don't even know all of the streets. My street, for example, contains about four long blocks with many circles. There are only a few vacant houses in my neighborhood. My neighborhood is both quiet and noisy. For example, there are about two kids in each house. My neighborhood is not exactly quiet, but polite. If someone is passing by in a car and you are in the yard, they will politely wave a hand to you. I believe that everyone would like to be closer neighbors if they had the time.

1 Is the paragraph all about one subject?

_____

2 Are there enough details or examples given to make clear to the reader exactly how the writer feels about the topic?

_____

3 Does the paragraph seem well planned?

_____

7 Read the following paragraph carefully, paying close attention to the subject of the paragraph and to its development with supporting detail.

Marion Estates is a quiet, peaceful, well-kept neighborhood with a low crime rate. The houses are made of wood, with flat tops, large yards, back yard gardens, trees, and clean streets. The residents are sociable but devote most of their time to themselves or social activities of their own. There are activities that the children play, such as football, baseball or basketball. The community is basically made up of nonprofessional middle class workers. There are some deficiencies in the neighborhood, such as a deficiency of home improvement and community planning.

1 Is this paragraph about one subject?

_____

2 Are there enough details or examples given to illustrate the topic fully?

_____

3 Does the paragraph seem well planned?

_____

These are the questions you should ask yourself while reading or writing your own paragraphs. If you answered no to any of the three questions, you should consider ways to revise your paragraph. How would you change the two paragraphs above?

_____

_____

_____

_____

_____

_____

Readings _____

Everybody Knows Benny Capalbo Invented the Grinder

W. G. Nicholson

8 The following four paragraphs are samples from the essay that begins on page 10. By reading these four paragraphs and answering the questions, you will prepare yourself to read and understand the entire essay more easily.

A well-stocked Italian grocery, then and now, contained all the ingredients for the mouth-watering <u>traditional</u> <u>grinder</u>. Properly made, it <u>consisted</u> of salami, provolone cheese, sliced tomatoes, and shredded lettuce all <u>liberally</u> sprinkled with salt, black pepper, and olive oil, between slices of Italian bread.

Reading for Meaning

1 Locate the underlined words in the paragraph, and reread the sentences in which they appear. Write your own definition of what the word means in that sentence. Use a dictionary if necessary.

traditional _____

grinder _____

consisted _____

liberally _____

Reading for Structure

2 What is the subject that the paragraph develops?

_____

3 Which sentence, then, is the topic sentence?

_____

4 Which is the support sentence?

_____

_____

_____

_____

9   The Italian bread, actually an <u>oblong</u>, submarine-shaped loaf, is <u>crucial</u> in the making of a "<u>real</u>" grinder. The loaf stays fresh for no more than a day or two. <u>Unglazed</u> and baked for 18 to 20 minutes in the 375 degree oven, one really has to chew hard, or "<u>grind</u>" away at it, to make progress.

Reading for Meaning

1 Locate the underlined words in the paragraph, and reread the sentences in which they appear. Write your own definition of what the word means in that sentence. Use a dictionary if necessary.

oblong _____

crucial _____

unglazed _____

"grind" _____

Reading for Structure

2 What is the subject that the paragraph develops?

_____

3 Which sentence, then, is the topic sentence?

_____

4 What idea is contained in the first support sentence?

_____

5 What idea is contained in the second support sentence?

_____

10   I <u>vividly</u> remember Benny's grocery in the early 1940s; by then it was located at 367 Bank Street, perhaps a half mile from its <u>original</u> location, open from 7 A.M. to 11 P.M. Outside, under an <u>awning,</u> stretched tables of fresh fruit. Inside, it was always cool and under-lighted, the air <u>redolent</u> of cheeses and salamis hanging by hooks from the ceiling.

Reading for Meaning

1 Locate the underlined words in the paragraph, and reread the sentences in which they appear. Write your own definition of what the word means in that sentence. Use a dictionary if necessary.

vividly_____

original_____

awning_____

redolent_____

Reading for Structure

2 What is the subject that the paragraph develops?

_____

3 Which sentence, then, is the topic sentence?

_____

4 There are four supporting ideas in this paragraph, all of which develop the topic sentence. Find the words in the paragraph that answer the following questions.

A. Where was Benny's store located?

_____

B. What times of day was the store open?

_____

C. What was the store like outside?

_____

8

D. What was the store like inside?

_____

5 There are two words used in the paragraph to describe the transition from the third supporting idea to the fourth. First the reader is _____ the store; then he moves _____ the store.

11   The shelves were stocked with <u>imported</u> Italian canned foods—<u>fiery</u> peppers, a variety of olive oils, antipasto, stuffed eggplants, green and black olives. One table was constantly piled high with <u>slabs</u> of dried, heavily salted cod. In one corner an <u>ancient</u> Coca-Cola cooler hummed steadily. Against a far wall was a refrigerated case, a long marble-topped table for making grinders, a cash register, and Benny himself.

Reading for Meaning

1 Locate the underlined words in the paragraph, and reread the sentences in which they appear. Write you own definition of what the word means in that sentence. Use a dictionary if necessary.

imported _____

fiery _____

slabs _____

ancient _____

Reading for Structure

2 What is the subject that the paragraph develops?

_____

3 Is there a topic sentence?

_____

4 Why is sentence 1 *not* the topic sentence?

_____

5 Write a topic sentence that contains the word *interior* as the subject for the whole paragraph.

_____

_____

_____

6 List the areas of the store described by the support sentences:

_____ , _____ , _____ , _____ ,

_____ .

7 List the transition words that explain where the last two areas

were located. _____ , _____ .

12 Now read the entire essay "Everybody Knows Benny Capalbo Invented the Grinder" with the sample paragraphs in place.

[1] Benny Capalbo was born in Salerno, Italy, about 1880. (He was never sure of the exact day or year of his birth.) But what is certain is that it was in Salerno as a young man that Benny operated a cafe in which he claimed he first <u>concocted</u> his special brand of sandwich.

[2] <u>Migrating</u> to America in 1913, Benny <u>eventually</u> landed in New London, a former whaling port of some 30,000 on Long Island Sound. By the early 1920s he owned a neighborhood grocery store at 18 Shaw Street in the heart of New London's Italian section. And although he had been making his special kind of sandwich for friends and relatives for some time, it was not until 1926 that he sold his first grinder.

[3] A well-stocked Italian grocery, then and now, contained all the ingredients for the mouth-watering traditional grinder. Properly made, it consisted of salami, provolone cheese, sliced tomatoes, and shredded lettuce all liberally sprinkled with salt, black pepper, and olive oil, between two slices of Italian bread.

[4] The Italian bread, actually an oblong, submarine-shaped loaf, is crucial in the making of a "real" grinder. The loaf stays fresh for no more than a day or two. Unglazed and baked for 18 to 20 minutes in a 375 degree oven, one really has to chew hard, or "grind" away at it, to make progress.

[5] Benny obtained his bread for the first grinders from the Italian-French bakery on Bank Street, right around the corner from his grocery. Both buildings, still housing a grocery and a bakery, remain in New London.

[6] I vividly remember Benny's grocery in the early 1940s; by

10

then it was located at 367 Bank Street, perhaps a half mile from its original location, open from 7 A.M. to 11 P.M. Outside, under an awning, stretched tables of fresh fruit. Inside, it was always cool and under-lighted, the air redolent of cheeses and salamis hanging by hooks from the ceiling.

[7] The shelves were stocked with imported Italian canned goods—fiery peppers, a variety of olive oils, antipasto, stuffed eggplants, green and black olives. One table was constantly piled high with slabs of dried, heavily salted cod. In one corner an ancient Coca-Cola cooler hummed steadily. Against a far wall was a refrigerated case, a long marble-topped table for making grinders, a cash register, and Benny himself.

[8] Benny was a short, stumpy man who wore the same flat cap indoors and out, winter or summer. His attire inevitably consisted of a dark cardigan, a greasy tie, a shirt with its collar points turned up, and a long white apron. Benny's appearance was anything but prepossessing, his demeanor even less so.

[9] A slow-moving man who seldom smiled, Benny was nevertheless a kind generous fellow, easily taken advantage of by neighbors and relatives. A customer would invariably wander around the store, eating a peach and then purchasing six others. Cheeses were constantly sampled, small bunches of grapes nibbled on. Virtually all of his customers literally ate away at the store's profits. And the profits, for a while anyway, were enormous.

[10] New London during World War II was a naval boom town. Over 12,000 sailors were attached to the Navy's huge Submarine Base; moreover, thousands of Coast Guardsmen were also stationed in the area. It was these hungry young servicemen who discovered Benny's grinders and fell in love with them.

[11] When the ships stopped at other ports, and when they finally went home, they found that grinders were unavailable. Then they would make suggestions to Italian grocery store operators and describe as well as they could the sandwich's ingredients. The end result was that the farther away the sailors moved from New London, the farther removed from Benny's grinders were the sandwiches they consumed. And the name changed—they became "Poor Boys" in Ohio, "Heroes" in New York City, "Hoagies" in the mid-Atlantic states—but Benny's sandwiches caught on throughout the nation.

[12] To satisfy the sailors' demands for grinders, New London's Submarine Base Commissary would daily order 400 to 500 of Benny's gastronomic creations. At one point the old grocery-man employed four women turning out the large sandwiches

to satisfy the Navy's demand as well as to <u>accommodate</u> the general public. And then other Italian grocery stores in New London quickly began turning out the sandwiches.

[13] But the boom time for grinders came to an end for Benny with increased competition in the area and the end of World War II when thousands of the Sub Base's sailors were discharged. Not long afterward Benny Capalbo lost his grocery as a result of poor management.

[14] Today, all the veteran grinder-makers in New London acknowledge their debt to Benny. "He could have been a millionaire, but he never did anything with it" is an often-heard lament accompanied by a shaking head. But then obtaining a U.S. patent on a sandwich would not have been an easy task for anyone, especially a slow-moving, <u>illiterate</u> Italian immigrant.

[15] When Benny Capalbo died 26 years ago, shortly after losing his store, his brief <u>obituary</u> noted that he had operated grocery stores in the Shaw and Bank Street areas of New London for a number of years; but <u>ironically</u> enough, there was no mention of his special contribution to American <u>culinary</u> life of the 20th century.

Reading for Meaning

1 Locate the underlined words in the essay, and reread the sentences in which they appear. Write your own definition of what the word means in that sentence. Use a dictionary if necessary.

concocted _____

migrating _____

eventually _____

prepossessing _____

demeanor _____

invariably _____

literally _____

gastronomic _____

accommodate _____

illiterate _____

obituary _____

ironically _____

culinary _____

Reading for Structure

2 Paragraphs 3 and 4 discuss the ingredients of a "grinder," and paragraphs 6 and 7 describe Benny's store. What function does paragraph 5 perform?

_____

_____

3 Why is paragraph 4 separated from paragraph 5? _____

_____

4 Why is paragraph 6 separated from paragraph 7? _____

_____

5 Write the topic sentence in paragraph 9. _____

_____

6 Paragraph 8 has no topic sentence. Write a topic sentence for the paragraph that contains the subject of the paragraph.

_____

_____

7 What is the subject of paragraph 10? _____

8 What is the subject of paragraph 11? _____

9 What is the subject of paragraph 12? _____

13

Comprehension Test

10 How old was Benny when he sold his first "grinder"? _____

11 What were the major ingredients of a "grinder"? _____

_____

12 Why was Benny's sandwich called a "grinder"? _____

_____

13 What is the main idea of the essay about Benny? _____

_____

14 Suggest an alternative title for the essay. _____

_____

15 What possible reason can be given for Benny's uncertainty about his age?

_____

16 Judging from the evidence in the article, tell what kind of person you think Benny Capalo was.

_____

17 What is the author's attitude toward his subject? Why?

_____

_____

Writing Assignments

18 Using paragraph 3 as a model, write a paragraph describing your favorite sandwich.

_____

_____

_____

_____

_____

_____

_____

_____

_____

_____

_____

_____

_____

_____

_____

_____

_____

_____

_____

_____

_____

_____

_____

_____

19 Using paragraph 8 as a model, write a paragraph describing someone you know well.

_____

_____

Readings _____

Violinist Isaac Stern Is a Unique Virtuoso: He Plays Both Music and Politics with Rare Skill

Joseph Roddy

13 The following two paragraphs are samples from the essay that begins on page 20. By reading these two paragraphs and answering the questions, you will prepare yourself to read and understand the entire essay more easily.

Over the years Stern has become one of the most powerful men in New York music, a position beyond argument after 1960 when his charm, political savvy and fund raising saved Carnegie Hall from destruction. To preserve music's most revered U.S. shrine, Stern accepted the presidency of the Carnegie Hall Corporation. "I have a reputation for making noises," he said at the time, "and people thought I could coordinate a lot of other noises into some kind of order." (Stern's reputation as a prodigious speaker on behalf of his causes gave rise long ago to this joke: One violin buff meets another in front of Carnegie Hall and says, "I just heard Isaac Stern; and the response is, "What did he say?") Stern's detractors complain that his position at Carnegie Hall gives him a hammerlock on classical music in America. Some aspiring young musicians who are not successful—and others who are neither successful nor young—say that Stern is an obstructionist who stands between them and fame. Exactly how he does this they find hard to explain. Stern replies to the charge: "They think I can wave a wand and get them instant managers, filled halls and lucrative careers, but I can't. And I can't use Carnegie Hall as a personal fief because it's not my personal property. It's a public place." For fear of sounding perhaps too ineffective, Stern does admit to a dollop of influence. "All I can do once in a while for a special talent is open a door."

Reading for Meaning

1 Locate the underlined words in the paragraph, and reread the sentences in which they appear. Write your own definition of what the word means in that sentence. Use a dictionary if necessary.

savvy _____

revered _____

prodigious _____

buff _____

detractors _____

aspiring _____

obstructionist _____

lucrative _____

fief _____

dollop _____

Reading for Structure

2 What is the topic that the paragraph develops? _____

_____

3 Is there a topic sentence? Which is the topic sentence? _____

_____

4 Find the supporting ideas in the paragraph that help illustrate the topic of Isaac Stern's power. Are there any supporting ideas that are unrelated to the topic?

_____

_____

_____

5 What transition words could have been used between sentences 5 and 6?

_____

_____

_____

_____

_____

14   Stern's principal teacher, Naoum Blinder, was the concert-master of the San Francisco Symphony. His single <u>renowned</u> student calls him a great man because he showed the young violinist how to teach himself. Isaac made his <u>debut</u> in San Francisco at 11, with Pierre Monteux conducting the city's symphony orchestra. Stern's New York debut when he was 17 was less than a triumph among the critics. "They admired my tone and <u>carped</u> at my <u>intonation</u>," Stern remembers. "The <u>consensus</u> was that I should go far. I did. I packed up my violin, convinced I didn't know my elbow from A flat, and went back to California." Six hard years of study later, Stern gave his first Carnegie Hall performance in 1943. He was launched into the thin ranks of the world's top <u>virtuosos</u>.

Reading for Meaning

1 Locate the underlined words in the paragraph, and reread the sentences in which they appear. Write your own definition of what the word means in that sentence. Use a dictionary if necessary.

renowned _____

debut _____

carped _____

intonation _____

consensus _____

virtuosos _____

Reading for Structure

2 List the supporting ideas in the paragraph. _____

_____

3 In as few words as possible, what is the topic that these supporting ideas develop?

_____

4 Using these words, write a topic sentence for this paragraph:

_____

_____

_____

Now read the entire essay "Violinist Isaac Stern Is a Unique Virtuoso" with the sample paragraphs in place.

15   [1] "When the history of violin playing is written, this will be called the Age of Heifetz." Isaac Stern said that one night recently while sipping a tall Scotch. Over his morning coffee a few days later, he said it again. Heifetz? Would Vladimir Horowitz be as generous—twice—about Arthur Rubinstein? Or Saul Bellow about Norman Mailer? Or Joe Namath about Ken Stabler?

[2] Maybe half of the violin lovers in the U.S. and Europe think that Isaac Stern is unsurpassable. Stern claims that's because most of them have not heard enough Jascha Heifetz. But the 75-year-old Heifetz rarely leaves his Beverly Hills home any more to concertize. That has made Stern, at 56, the virtuoso for concert managers who want to boast that they have engaged (for about $10,000 a night) the world's highest-priced fiddler.

[3] When he has a Guarnerius tucked under his jowled left jaw and a Tourte bow gripped in his thick-fingered right hand, Stern may in fact be Mr. Second Fiddle to Heifetz, as he insists. But wherever music and political power overlap on the world stage, Stern is the undisputed master. When music historians tell of violinists who did more than flex their bow arms, this will be called the Age of Stern.

[4] During the cold war Stern was the first American soloist to tour the Soviet concert circuit—even before there was a cultural exchange treaty. In Moscow he conducted a long, spirited

20

dialogue on the subject with Nikita Khrushchev that helped create a climate in both countries for acceptance of the 1958 treaty.

[5] Then, in 1967, Stern was the first American artist to break off relations with the Kremlin. He sent word to the Ministry of Culture that he would not return until Soviet artists could come and go as freely as he does and perform in any country they cared to, including—and especially—Israel. (Stern has not set foot in the Soviet Union for nearly 10 years.)

[6] His defense of Israel on the cultural battlefronts of the world has made him one of that country's major heroes. Whenever Israel mobilizes, Stern heads for Tel Aviv. In the 1973 war, for example, he went into the desert and performed as many as six concerts a day to raise morale. His favorite work was a 12-minute version of the Mendelssohn concerto into which he slipped strains of the national anthem, *Hatikvah*. When Israel was barred by UNESCO from its European regional group and cut off from cultural aid in 1974, Stern persuaded conductors Leonard Bernstein, Pierre Boulez, Julius Rudel, Thomas Schippers, and Michael Tilson Thomas to refuse to participate in any UNESCO events. The musicians' boycott, along with pressure from many other sources, brought an end to the ban last year.

[7] Israel has played an important role in Stern's politics, his music, and even his family life. He originally visited the country in 1949, taking along his first wife, ballerina Nora Kaye. After they were divorced, he met his Berlin-born second wife, Vera, in Jerusalem in 1951. Their daughter, Shira, 21, a Brown University student, is now spending her junior year in Israel. Whenever her father flies in, as he does from three to five times a year, the U.S. ambassador there sizes up the receptions pressed on Stern and is reminded that his own diplomatic credentials are no match for the fiddler's.

[8] Stern's connections in Washington are equally impressive. He has been playing chamber music for years with former Supreme Court Justice Abe Fortas, a skilled violinist. When Stern was invited to speak to the National Press Club last November—the invitation itself a recognition of his political influence—his friend Henry Kissinger turned up in the audience. It is hardly a musician's job to appeal for more Phantoms for the Israeli Air Force; nonetheless, few accredited ambassadors represent their countries as eloquently and effectively as Stern does his adopted promised land.

[9] Stern was born in 1920 in Kremenets, a tiny town in the Soviet Ukraine. It is 350 miles northwest of Odessa, which fact and <u>folklore</u> have <u>hallowed</u> as the place Soviet Jews should be born to be great musicians. Nathan Milstein, Boris Kroyt, and Simon Barere, who left the Soviet Union to live in this country, were born in Odessa, as were David Oistrakh and Emil Gilels, who stayed home. Stern once memorably defined U.S.–Soviet cultural exchange: "They send us their Jews from Odessa, and we send them ours."

[10] Stern's mother studied singing at the Imperial Conservatory in St. Petersburg. His father was a painter without enough buyers, and the family emigrated to San Francisco when their only son was 10 months old. He started piano when he was 6 and switched to the violin at 8 because the boy across the street was taking lessons on the instrument.

[11] Stern's principal teacher, Naoum Blinder, was the concertmaster of the San Francisco Symphony. His single renowned student calls him a great man because he showed the young violinist how to teach himself. Isaac made his debut in San Francisco at 11, with Pierre Monteux conducting the city's symphony orchestra. Stern's New York debut when he was 17 was less than a triumph among the critics. "They admired my tone and carped at my intonation," Stern remembers. "The consensus was that I should go far. I did. I packed up my violin, convinced I didn't know my elbow from A flat, and went back to California." Six hard years of study later, Stern gave his first Carnegie Hall performance in 1943. He was launched into the thin ranks of the world's top virtuosos.

[12] Over the years Stern has become one of the most powerful men in New York music, a position beyond argument after 1960 when his charm, political savvy, and fund raising saved Carnegie Hall from destruction. To preserve music's most revered U.S. shrine, Stern accepted the presidency of the Carnegie Hall Corporation. "I have a reputation for making noises," he said at the time, "and people thought I could coordinate a lot of other noises into some kind of order." (Stern's reputation as a prodigious speaker on behalf of his causes gave rise long ago to this joke: One violin buff meets another in front of Carnegie Hall and says, "I just heard Isaac Stern"; and the response is, "What did he say?") Stern's detractors complain that his position at Carnegie Hall gives him a hammerlock on classical music in America. Some aspiring young musicians who are not successful—and others who are neither successful nor young— say that Stern is an obstructionist who stands between them and fame. Exactly how he does this they find hard to explain. Stern replies to the charge: "They think I can wave a wand and get them instant managers, filled halls and lucrative careers, but I can't. And I can't use Carnegie Hall as a personal fief

because it's not my personal property. It's a public place." For fear of sounding perhaps too ineffective, Stern does admit to a dollop of influence. "All I can do once in a while for a special talent is open a door."

[13] He is <u>excessively</u> modest. He opened an important door 10 years ago for the young Israeli violinist Pinchas Zukerman, and again a few years later for the even younger Israeli violinist Itzakh Perlman. For Zukerman it <u>eventually</u> meant a recording contract with Columbia, for Perlman with RCA. Some of their albums these days are selling faster than Stern's (he records for Columbia), and their fees for <u>recitals</u> are climbing too. While his Carnegie Hall Corporation can still afford them, Stern is glad to have Perlman and Zukerman join his annual chamber music festival, a two-week series of programs billed as concerts by "Isaac Stern and Friends."

[14] At Carnegie Hall a few weeks ago, Stern listened to a student orchestra from all over the U.S. give a high-energy performance of Beethoven's Triple Concerto. Its violin and piano soloists, Shlomo Mintz and Yefim Bronfman, were young Soviet-born Israelis brought to New York by the American-Israel Cultural Foundation, which some Israelis regard as a Stern family charity. On stage between Mintz and Bronfman was a young Chinese <u>cellist</u>, born in Paris and named Yo-Yo Ma. Had talent scout Stern been unable to find a third Israeli to play the Beethoven? "There was no need," a friend of Stern explained. "Isaac knows that Yo-Yo plays Jewish."

[15] In the 1940s Stern landed his first Hollywood job as the hands for John Garfield, who was portraying a young violinist struggling for the kind of success that Stern had only recently managed at Carnegie Hall. "My hands were shaved so they'd look like Garfield's," Stern says, "and they had me teach him how to hold a fiddle. They made movies of me for him to study." Stern looked at the films too and was appalled at his image. "I came out looking like a badly fried and battered haddock."

[16] Since then—face, hands and nimble feet—he played the role of the great Belgian violinist Eugène Ysaye in 1953's *Tonight We Sing*, about the life of impresario Sol Hurok. Not even his hands are visible in the movie version of *Fiddler on the Roof*, where the poignant solo violin on the soundtrack is Stern's.

[17] In 1973 he accompanied Margot Fonteyn on the stage of the Metropolitan Opera House, where he played Tchaikovsky while she danced a scene from *Swan Lake*. Two years ago he went to Carnegie Hall in grief and sent Hurok, his old friend and manager, to his grave with Bach.

[18] Getting the head of the Stern house off to France and Israel for concerts early this month turned into a family project. Father dictated last-minute letters into a tape recorder perched on the basin while he shaved. His violin-playing son Michael, 17, carefully packed the Guarnerius, the four bows and the extra strings (Stern does not carry a spare violin when he travels) while his younger brother David, 13, a pianist, carried the luggage into the elevator of the apartment, which overlooks Central Park. Mrs. Stern went to get the family station wagon from the garage. Her husband took the wheel and drove to Kennedy Airport where he immediately picked up a lounge phone to call Horowitz and Milstein just to stay in touch. Without telephones, his manager once told him he would live 10 years longer—and have more time to practice, his friends say. "I have played more wrong notes than I hope you will ever know in your lives," he told a worshipful crowd of young musicians not long ago. "I'm an old and well-wounded warrior."

[19] What gives out first on a fiddler, he has been asked. "The bow arm," he said, "and you're a real son of a bitch for asking." All in all, however, Isaac Stern seems completely satisfied with the frenzied life he leads.

[20] He talks about staying power, and brings a conversation dealing with his mortality to a close, typically, with a joke. "You know what happens to old fiddlers, don't you?" he asks, then supplies the answer with a twinkle: "They just fake away."

Reading for Meaning

1 Locate the underlined words in the essay, and reread the sentences in which they appear. Write your own definition of what the word means in that sentence. Use a dictionary if necessary.

unsurpassable _____

folklore _____

hallowed _____

memorably _____

cultural _____

emigrated _____

excessively _____

eventually _____

recitals _____

cellist _____

Reading for Structure

2 Just as the supporting ideas of a paragraph must be planned
and ordered, so must the paragraphs themselves be in some
sort of planned, logical order when they are placed in an essay.
For example, why are the two example paragraphs (12 and 13)
reordered as they are in the essay?

_____

_____

_____

3 What are the support ideas in paragraph 12? _____

_____

4 What topic is developed in paragraph 12? _____

_____

5 Write a topic sentence for paragraph 12 that uses the topic word
as the subject of the sentence.

_____

_____

_____

6 What is the general topic that paragraphs 10, 11, and 12 develop?

_____

_____

_____

_____

7 What is the topic of paragraph 14? _____

_____

8 What is the topic of paragraph 15? _____

_____

9 Find the transition sentence that separates the discussion of Stern's helping younger artists from the discussion of a recent performance.

_____

_____

Comprehension Test

10 When was Stern born? _____

11 Where was he born? _____

12 Name four musicians who were born in Odessa, near Kremenets, the birthplace of Stern.   _____, _____,

_____, _____.

13 When did Stern make his performing debut? _____

14 When did Stern first perform at Carnegie Hall? _____

15 What important organization is Stern associated with?

_____

16 Name the two violinists Stern has "launched" since he has been president of the Carnegie Hall Corporation.

_____, _____.

17 What was Stern's early background like? _____

_____

18 What was his debut like? _____

_____

_____

19 What is "Isaac Stern and Friends"? _____

_____

20 Why is Stern's presidency of the Carnegie Corporation important?

_____

21 Explain the joke in the last paragraph. _____

_____

_____

22 Who is Naoum Blinder? _____

23 Now that you have read the essay, what do you think the title of the essay means?

_____

_____

Writing Assignments

24 How much do you know about the life of your favorite musician? Write a paragraph describing that background.

_____

_____

_____

_____

_____

_____

_____

_____

_____

_____

_____

_____

_____

_____

_____

_____

25 Write a paragraph describing the kind of music you like. Use good, relevant supporting detail; give examples or names of specific songs by specific artists.

_____

_____

_____

_____

_____

_____

_____

_____

_____

_____

_____

_____

_____

_____

_____

_____

_____

_____

_____

_____

_____

_____

Readings

Strivers' Row:
The Good Life in
Harlem

Stephen Birmingham

16 The following three paragraphs are samples from the essay that begins on page 35. By reading these three paragraphs and answering the questions, you will prepare yourself to read and understand the entire essay more easily.

In the earliest days of New York, Harlem was a <u>rural</u> area of fields and farms, where old New York white families had properties. What is now Strivers' Row once belonged to such families as the Cadwalladers, Lynches, Pinckneys, and Delanceys. As the city grew, Harlem became a kind of middle-class suburb, where real-estate values were somewhat <u>depressed</u>, since Harlem was considered a difficult place to get to. In 1891, a builder named David H. King, Jr., <u>commissioned</u> a number of leading New York architects—including McKim, Mead & White and its famous partner Stanford White—to design a series of elegant, four-story row houses on West 138th and 139th streets between Seventh and Eighth avenues, to be called the *King Model Houses.* The houses had handsome entrances and <u>facades</u>, <u>casement</u> windows and balconies, <u>balustraded</u> roofs. Behind the houses were courtyards, gardens, and fountains, connected by an interior alleyway that ran the length of both blocks. The houses were built of brick, <u>terra-cotta</u>, and Belleville brownstone, a special stone gathered from the banks of the Passaic River. The King Houses were to be, according to Mr. King's sale <u>brochure</u>, for "millionaires." At first, they were—white Christian millionaires, such as the first Randolph Hearst.

Reading for Meaning

1 Locate the underlined words in the paragraph, and reread the sentences in which they appear. Write your own definition of what the word means in that sentence. Use a dictionary if necessary.

rural _____

depressed _____

commissioned _____

facades _____

casement _____

balustraded _____

terra-cotta _____

brochure _____

Reading for Structure:

2 What is the topic of this paragraph?_____

3 Write a topic sentence that contains the controlling idea—the subject and the assertion made about it—for the paragraph.

_____

_____

4 In an essay on Strivers' Row as it looks now, where do you think this paragraph would be placed?

_____

_____

_____

17   In the early 1920s, one by one, the King Model Houses began to be sold to blacks who were, for the most part, professional people and therefore <u>relatively</u> <u>affluent</u>—doctors, lawyers, and educators. And the new black residents of these houses decided, at the outset, that their two streets would not be sucked into the <u>burgeoning</u> slum beyond. The trees were <u>tended</u>, the hedges clipped, the stone vases and window boxes were kept filled with flowering plants. Entrance railings and balustrades were painted; brass doorknobs and knockers were polished. Gardens and courtyards were maintained. Each neighbor tried so hard to compete with the others for the best-clipped shrubbery, the best polished brasswork, the best-washed steps, and the prettiest garden that the two <u>parallel</u> blocks were humorously given the name "Strivers' Row."

Reading for Meaning

1 Locate the underlined words in the paragraph, and reread the sentences in which they appear. Write your own definition of what the word means in that sentence. Use a dictionary if necessary.

relatively _____

affluent _____

burgeoning _____

tended _____

parallel _____

Reading for Structure

2 What is the topic developed in the paragraph?

_____

3 Is there a topic sentence? Why?

_____

4 What are the supporting ideas presented in the paragraph?

_____

5 List the details needed to support the idea that Strivers' Row homes were maintained better than the surrounding homes.

_____

_____

_____

_____

6 Are these details ordered in any particular way? _____

_____

7 Notice the listing in the final sentence. Is this list in the same order as the listing of details in the middle of the paragraph?

_____   This kind of sentence, which refers back to main ideas, is a concluding sentence.

18   Of course, what was intended as a shining example to other blacks of what could be done to create a pleasant neighborhood very quickly had the opposite effect. The more attractive and <u>manicured</u> Strivers' Row became, the more it found itself the object of <u>mockery</u>, jealousy, and bitter <u>hostility</u> among the other blacks of Harlem. A black playwright named Abram Hill, who died in 1939 and who wrote a play about the Row, used to recall how he had to pass through the neighborhood on his way to school and developed, with no real knowledge of the people who lived there, a terrible <u>resentment</u> of these blacks who clearly lived better than he—just from passing the <u>grilled</u> entrances and looking up at the carefully curtained windows of the Row.

Reading for Meaning

1 Locate the underlined words in the paragraph, and reread the sentences in which they appear. Write your own definition of what the word means in that sentence. Use a dictionary if necessary.

manicured _____

mockery _____

hostility _____

resentment _____

grilled _____

Reading for Structure

2 Is there a topic sentence in this paragraph? Where?

_____

3 What one example is used to illustrate the resentment other Harlem residents felt toward Strivers' Row?

_____

_____

_____

4 What sentence tells the reader that Abram Hill's resentment was typical?

_____

_____

5 In an essay on Strivers' Row, should this paragraph be before or after the paragraph that describes the maintenance of the houses?

_____

_____

_____

Now read the entire essay "Strivers' Row: The Good Life in Harlem" with the sample paragraphs in place.

19

[1] "The social life was gay and wonderful, with luncheons, bridge parties, and formal, white-tie dances. Everyone seemed to have everything—cars, boats, and summer homes. We lived without a care in the world." The speaker is not a wealthy dowager reminiscing about growing up in Southampton. It is an 82-year-old black woman, Mrs. Gerri Major of New York, and she is recalling what life was like for her as a girl in Harlem. Mrs. Major, who for years served as *Ebony's* society editor, is not, of course, talking about *all* of Harlem—just that tiny pocket of citified pride and self-assurance in the heart of Harlem known as Strivers' Row, an area of Manhattan that most white New Yorkers do not know exists and that few have ever seen. Furthermore, while the rest of Harlem has changed drastically since Mrs. Major's girlhood, Strivers' Row has remained pretty much the same.

[2] In the earliest days of New York, Harlem was a rural area of fields and farms, where old New York white families had properties. What is now Strivers' Row once belonged to such families as the Cadwalladers, Lynches, Pinckneys, and Delanceys. As the city grew, Harlem became a kind of middle-class suburb, where real-estate values were somewhat depressed, since Harlem was considered a difficult place to get to. In 1891, a builder named David H. King, Jr., commissioned a number of leading New York architects—including McKim, Mead & White and its famous partner Stanford White—to design a series of elegant, four-story row houses on West 138th and 139th streets between Seventh and Eighth avenues, to be called the King Model Houses. The houses had handsome entrances and facades, casement windows and balconies, balustraded roofs. Behind the houses were courtyards, gardens, and fountains, connected by an interior alleyway that ran the length of both blocks. The houses were built of brick, terracotta, and Belleville brownstone, a special stone gathered from the banks of the Passaic River. The King Houses were to be, according to Mr. King's sale brochure, for "millionaires." At first, they were—white Christian millionaires such as the first Randolph Hearst.

[3] But in the late nineteenth century, as huge migrations of Russian and Polish Jews flooded into the city, fleeing the pogroms of Eastern Europe, Harlem became predominantly Jewish. By 1910, an overwhelming majority of the people who lived between 110th Street and 155th Street and between the East and Hudson rivers were either foreign-born or had foreign-born parents. Russian Jews dominated the 1910 census figures.

Next came the Italians, then the Irish, then the Germans, then the English, Hungarians, Czechs, and others coming from the Austro-Hungarian Empire. In addition, there were 75,000 native whites and only 50,000 blacks.

[4] Blacks did not arrive in New York in any large numbers until after World War I, and they followed the lead of foreign immigrants and moved to Harlem. Most were from the South, and most were poor. As blacks moved in, the Jews moved out —north into the Bronx or, if they could afford it, to the south shore of Long Island. They remained, however, in many cases as landlords.

[5] In the early 1920s, one by one, the King Model Houses began to be sold to blacks who were, for the most part, professional people and therefore relatively affluent—doctors, lawyers, and educators. And the new black residents of these houses decided, at the outset, that their two streets would not be sucked into the burgeoning slum beyond. The trees were tended, the hedges clipped, the stone vases and window boxes were kept filled with flowering plants. Entrance railings and balustrades were painted; brass doorknobs and knockers were polished. Gardens and courtyards were maintained. Each neighbor tried so hard to compete with the others for the best-clipped shrubbery, the best-polished brasswork, the best-washed steps, and the prettiest garden that the two parallel blocks were humorously given the name "Strivers' Row."

[6] "It could have been done in other parts of Harlem, too," says one longtime resident of the Row. "There used to be many lovely old streets up here. Even when a house is broken up into tiny apartments, the facade and the appearance of the neighborhood can be kept up. It doesn't take that much money or that much time just to give doorways and frames a regular coat of paint. Garbage doesn't have to be thrown in the streets or down air shafts. It's people who don't care who create slums, and then the slums create people who don't care. It becomes a vicious circle. Attractive surroundings help make attractive people."

[7] Of course, what was intended as a shining example to other blacks of what could be done to create a pleasant neighborhood very quickly had the opposite effect. The more attractive and manicured Strivers' Row became, the more it found itself the object of mockery, jealousy, and bitter hostility among the other blacks of Harlem. A black playwright named Abram Hill, who died in 1939 and who wrote a play about the Row, used to recall how he had to pass through the neighborhood on his way to school and developed, with no real knowledge of the people who lived there, a terrible resentment of these blacks,

who clearly lived better than he—just from passing the grilled entrances and looking up at the carefully curtained windows of the Row.

[8] "It's as though the rest of Harlem wanted to force us into becoming a ghetto," says one Row resident. "They developed this blind hatred of us as society snobs. We weren't snobs. We just wanted to live in a nice neighborhood. There was no way to reach those people, but we resisted them. We've held on." In resisting, Strivers' Row became more <u>insular</u>, withdrawn into itself, more inbred, proud, and prejudiced against ghetto blacks.

[9] When the first black families began moving to the Row, there was the usual <u>flurry</u> of panic selling, and three- and four-story townhouses would be picked up for bargain prices. James W. Banks, who is president of the 138th Street Block Association and an associate administrator of the Board of Elections—his father was one of New York's first black dentists—has lived on the Row nearly all of his 54 years and recalls, "We were the sixth black family to move in. My father bought our twelve-room house for $9,000." Today, Row houses sell in the $50,000 range. Another early Row resident was Dr. Louis T. Wright, the first black doctor at Harlem Hospital and later its chief of surgery, whose family lived on the Row for 32 years. Then there was Dr. Charles H. Roberts, another early New York black dentist, and Vertner W. Tandy, the first black architect to be licensed in New York State, and Samuel J. Battle, Manhattan's first black police lieutenant.

[10] At this writing, the oldest resident of Strivers' Row is probably 88-year-old Mrs. Robert Braddicks, the widow of a banker and a real-estate broker. Mrs. Braddicks, who also maintains a summer-and-weekend home in New Jersey, had, during her 56-year residence, become a <u>symbol</u> of the <u>enclave's stability</u>. But this year, yielding to the wishes of her children and grandchildren, she will finally leave her fourteen-room house on West 138th Street to move to an apartment in Peter Cooper village. "I hate to do it," she says, "this has been my home so long, but it's just too much house for a woman alone."

[11] At one point, Strivers' Row was a popular address for successful show-business personalities. Fletcher Henderson, W. C. Handy, Stepin Fetchit, Eubie Blake, Noble Sissle, Flannery Muller, and Sidney Bechet all had homes on the Row at one time or another. More recently, Strivers' Row has become popular with young executives, businessmen, and professional people who work in Harlem, such as Jean Wade, the advertising director of the *Amsterdam News,* Walter Legall, who is an officer with a computer firm, and educator Charles L. Sanders. Booker T. Washington III, an architect, has become a Row resident, as has New York Supreme Court Justice Oliver Sutton. Today, there is a long waiting list for houses on the Row.

[12] If anything, Strivers' Row today is more attractive and house-proud than ever. In 1967, New York's Landmarks Preservation Commission declared the Strivers' Row houses a landmark, meaning that no exterior changes can be made to any of the houses without the permission of the commission. This distinction has added to Row residents' feelings of security and self-satisfaction. Still, Strivers' Row remains a tiny island of comfort and affluence in the middle of a seething sea of desperation, danger, and urban indifference. Step around the corner, and you are in Harlem's lowest depths. In this situation, the Row has become a prime target for Harlem's criminal element. Mrs. Braddick's house has been burglarized twice. Still, with the help of two powerful neighborhood associations, Row residents have been able to secure extra police protection for their little Andorra (it hasn't hurt to have judges and retired police officers living on the Row). Elaborate burglar-alarm systems have been installed, along with powerful lights to illuminate the once-shadowy backyards at night. And a group of Row residents, consisting mostly of retirees, has been organized as a volunteer watch force "to keep an eye on things." Thus Strivers' Row hangs on. "This has been a nice place to live for over 50 years," says one resident. "It's going to remain that way for another 50."

[13] Strivers' Row's two block association have rigid rules which are rigidly enforced; no trash or litter is to be thrown in streets; hedges are to be kept uniformly clipped; brasswork is to be polished; children are not to play in the streets; no peddlers or solicitors are to be admitted through front entrances; all pickups and deliveries are to made through back entrances, courts, and alleyways; residents should beautify gardens and window boxes and replace dead or ailing trees; and so on. In its pride, Strivers' Row has become extraordinarily exclusive. In a survey conducted by the Landmarks Preservation Commission, it was noted that 41 percent of the people living on Strivers' Row socialize only with their immediate neighbors on the Row. A mere 12 percent venture outside the area for any social activity. Nearly half do not socialize at all.

[14] Recently there have been a few voices raised along the Row that have questioned its encapsulated, ostrich-like existence, that have suggested that Strivers' Row is painfully out of

touch with the reality of modern times. Instead of an island, Strivers' Row might step out of its cocoon and become a responsible, involved leader of the total Harlem community. One such man is James Banks, Jr., who has tried to move the little community outward into the affairs and terrible problems of the much larger one. But so far he is in the minority. Others, happy as they are, see Strivers' Row as a symbol of what black people could have done with Harlem if they had cared enough, been bright enough, worked hard enough. Why didn't blacks do it in other neighborhoods? "Shiftless, lazy," sniffs one Row woman. "They're no good, those people. No good at all."

Reading for Meaning

1 Locate the underlined words in the essay, and reread the sentences in which they appear. Write your own definition of what the word means in that sentence. Use a dictionary if necessary.

reminiscing_____

citified_____

drastically_____

predominantly_____

census_____

insular_____

flurry_____

symbol_____

enclave_____

stability_____

distinction_____

affluence_____

seething_____

element (criminal)_____

illuminate_____

The words in the left-hand column are underlined in the essay. Reread the sentences in which they appear and pick, from the choices at the right, the word that is closest in meaning. Circle your answer.

rigid	stiff	strict	hardened
ailing	sick	dead	thriving
exclusive	banished	open-ended	limited
venture (verb)	go forth	undertaking	adventure
encapsulated	captured	shut in	opened

Reading for Structure

2 In paragraph 11, what is the topic illustrated?

_____

3 Why is the first sentence in paragraph 11 *not* the topic sentence?

_____

4 Why is the third sentence *not* the topic sentence?

_____

5 Write a topic sentence for paragraph 11 that will include both the ideas that Strivers' Row has become home for show-business personalities and for young professional people.

_____

_____

_____

6 In paragraph 13, two main supporting ideas are used. What are they?

_____

_____

7 Which sentence is the topic sentence in paragraph 13? Why?

_____

_____

8 The last paragraph lists possible roles for Strivers' Row in the life of Harlem. What are they?

_____

_____

_____

Comprehension Test

9 Which four rich families originally owned the rural area that became known as Harlem?

_____ , _____ , _____ , _____

10 What did David H. King, Jr., do?

_____

11 Which important newspaper publisher moved to Strivers' Row with the first white "millionaires"?_____

12 Name three successful black professional people who live in Strivers' Row today. _____ , _____ , _____ .

13 Name three successful black show-business personalities who lived in Strivers' Row in the early days.

_____ , _____ , _____ .

14 List five rules that the current inhabitants of Strivers' Row have made to keep the Row from becoming a slum.

————————————————, ————————————————,

————————————————, ————————————————,

————————————————.

15 What types of blacks came to the Row in the early 1920s?

——

16 How did Strivers' Row get its name?

——

——

——

17 What effect has Strivers' Row had on other blacks in Harlem?

——

18 Strivers' Row began as a white rural area and is today an exclusive black neighborhood. List the five steps in the Row's development from rural white to urban black.

——

——

——

——

19 List four precautions the inhabitants of the Row have taken to curb crime.

————————————————————————

————————————————————————

————————————————————————

————————————————————————

20 What is the attitude of people who live on the Row toward other sections of Harlem?

_____

_____

_____

21 Summarize Mrs. Gerri Major's view of Strivers' Row.

_____

_____

_____

_____

_____

22 What is Strivers' Row like today?

_____

_____

_____

_____

_____

23 Why do the people of Strivers' Row not want to get involved in helping the surrounding sections of Harlem?

_____

_____

_____

_____

24 Often an author will use a particular word to illustrate his tone (or attitude) toward his subject. Refer to the title of the essay. Which words in the title suggest that the author does not have the usual attitude toward Harlem?

Writing Assignments

25 Write a paragraph describing your own neighborhood, using details that will make the way you feel about your neighborhood clear for your reader.

_____

_____

_____

_____

_____

_____

_____

_____

_____

_____

_____

26 Using your library if necessary, write a paragraph describing
the most outstanding accomplishments of some of the show-
business personalities mentioned in paragraph 11.

_____

_____

_____

_____

_____

_____

_____

_____

_____

_____
_____
_____
_____
_____
_____
_____
_____
_____
_____
_____
_____
_____

27 How do you think the people of Strivers' Row should feel about the rest of Harlem? Write a paragraph giving your opinion and your reasons for holding that opinion.

_____
_____
_____
_____
_____
_____
_____
_____
_____

_____

_____

_____

_____

_____

_____

_____

_____

_____

_____

_____

_____

_____

_____

2 Chronological Arrangement of Detail

In the first chapter, you read paragraphs that were developed with specific details. These details can be arranged in many different ways; the first chapter includes spatial, chronological, and climactic paragraphs. Some kinds of subjects are best written about with certain kinds of arrangements. For example, *chronological* or *time* organization is used to describe events, incidents, or processes such as baking a cake, changing a tire, writing a paragraph, or directions to a party. In such paragraphs, the supporting ideas or details are arranged *in the order in which they occur* or, in the case of a paragraph of directions, *in the order in which they should occur*.

The transition words used in this sort of paragraph are words that mention specific times (*at one o'clock*, *at two o'clock, after a while*, *during the next six months* . . .) or words that indicate time relationships among the supporting ideas (*first, next, finally, later, when, then* . . .).

1 Read this sample paragraph, following its organization very closely by underlining transitions and numbering each supporting idea.

The most important thing that has happened to me in the past two years would have to be going back to school. Because I quit high school in the tenth grade, I can truthfully say my education was lacking. After quitting school I fiddled around for about a year, but after a year was up, I realized I would never get a decent job; so I took a welding course at the Area Technical School. After completing the course, I accepted a job at a local Iron and Steel Works. I had worked about five months at minimal pay when I decided there had to be a better way of making a living. I decided to try my luck at getting a G.E.D. certificate. I passed the test and then took the S.A.T. Now I am going to college and the future looks a lot brighter.

1 Which sentence is the topic sentence? _____

2 Does the final sentence add any specific supporting detail?

_____

3 How many supporting ideas are there? _____

List them. _____

4 List the transition words and phrases used in the paragraph.

_____

5 Are any of the supporting ideas not in the order in which they occurred?

_____

2 Read the following paragraph, paying close attention to the ordering of the events.

The most important thing that has happened to me lately is learning to play tennis. When I went to the tennis courts, I was hitting the ball from one court to the next, over fences, and into graveyards. I said to myself, "I'll never learn this crazy game." I tried harder and harder, but I could see no progress, and I became discouraged. I went to see a tennis pro, who encouraged me to work on the basic elements. I worked on basics such as stance and grip. It was boring work, but I realized one day that I was able to make the shots I never thought I could make.

1 Did you notice that, although it is arranged correctly in chronological order, the paragraph seems unconnected? Now read it again, inserting these transition phrases where you think they would be appropriate:

at first   for almost six months
day after day   finally
then one day

2 Which of the following sentences would make the best concluding sentence for the paragraph? Circle your answer below.

    A. All the various aspects of tennis are important to me.

    B. In addition, the tennis pro gave me some pointers on mental
attitude.

    C. Now that I've learned the basics, I love the game of tennis.

    D. I also like baseball now.

3 Put these notes about an automobile accident into chronological order by placing numbers in the blanks. Begin with number
1 for the first detail.

_____ leave driveway at home, feeling good
_____ ambulance arrives
_____ police arrive
_____ screeching brakes
_____ emergency room
_____ old VW can't stop at light, goes through
_____ goes to court in about a year
_____ tickets for both of us
_____ nose broken against steering wheel
_____ bend shift knob
_____ old man screams "whiplash!"
_____ approaching intersection in my Ford

3 Write a paragraph, using these notes. Write your topic sentence
here.

_____

_____

_____

_____

_____

4   Put this jumbled paragraph into chronological order by placing numbers in the blanks.

_____ Two policemen got out of their car, walked up to my house, and knocked on the door.

_____ They had a warrant for Bill Bandler, of 2216 Kelvin Road.

_____ Since that night, I always check to make sure that the nine stays a nine!

_____ The first time I ever had an encounter with the law was about one o'clock in the morning.

_____ Finally, we discovered that the nine in our address, 2219, had fallen upside down to look like the six in 2216.

_____ My sister opened the door and there they were, uniforms, guns, and all.

_____ As we tried to explain that they had the wrong house, they looked at the warrant, at the house number, and back at us as if we were hiding Bill Bandler in the kitchen.

5   Read this paragraph; notice its organization.

    The most important thing that has happened to me was becoming a licensed nurse. This was very important to me; all my life I've wanted to become a nurse. When the chance came to become a nurse under the CETA program, I was the happiest person in the world. I studied hard all year long and wasn't sure I was going to pass the boards to become licensed, but I did pass and was very happy.

1   Which is the topic sentence? _____

2   List the transition words and phrases you found in the paragraph. _____

3   Is the paragraph organized chronologically? _____

4   Is there enough detail to convince you that the topic sentence is true? _____

5 List the main supporting ideas in the paragraph; put them in chronological order.

_____

_____

_____

_____

6 What other details could the author of this paragraph have included?

_____

_____

_____

_____

6 Read this paragraph carefully.

Late one Saturday afternoon I was trying to make it downtown before the stores closed and pick up a package I had

ordered. I was driving at about 50 miles per hour _____
I saw a police car coming in the opposite direction. I tried to

slow down, _____ they went down a block, turned around, and turned on their flashing light. I pulled off the road

and began looking for my license; _____ the policeman

was at my window, asking if I knew I was speeding. _____

_____the stores were closed.

1 Now read the paragraph again, inserting the appropriate transition in each blank position in the paragraph.

By the time he finished his lecture and wrote the ticket,
but
when
by then

2 Which is the topic sentence? _____

3 Which of the following would be the best concluding sentence

for this paragraph? Why? _____

   A. That was all on a Saturday afternoon.

   B. So I couldn't pick up my package.

   C. The ticket was only for five dollars.

   D. There I sat, with a ticket worth more than the package I had
      been speeding downtown to pick up.

   E. Ever since that day, I've made it a rule to never buy anything
      that isn't in stock everyday.

7 Read the following paragraph carefully.

    A friend of mine stole a half gallon of Scotch, and because
we were only fourteen, we sat in his brother's Plymouth out in
the alley while we drank the whole half gallon. A neighbor saw
my friend fall out of the car flat on his face. She called the
police, saying someone was dropping a body in the alley behind
her house. A policeman came around the corner of the garage,
pulling his gun and yelling. Because I was both scared and
drunk, I tried to run, but he caught me and took me to a waiting
car. I sobered up at the Youth Development Center. My dad and
my godfather came out and picked me up.

1 Write a topic sentence for the paragraph.

_____

_____

_____

2 Where should the following transition phrases be inserted in
the paragraph?

It all started when _____

The next morning _____

The rest of that afternoon and night _____

At about the same time _____

Within minutes _____

Immediately _____

3 Which of these sentences would be the best concluding sentence for this paragraph? Circle your answer.

  A. Then they beat me with a stick.

  B. You should have seen the looks on their faces.

  C. That was the end of my drinking for quite some time.

  D. That's why I prefer bourbon to Scotch.

  E. And I have had many other encounters with liquor and police, often at the same time.

Readings_____

James Dickey's Glory

James Dickey

8 The following paragraph is a sample from the essay that begins on page 57. By reading this paragraph and answering the questions, you will prepare yourself to read and understand the entire essay more easily.

When I suited up for the finals, though, I was ready. I felt that I had come to run. It was a cool night and there were several hundred people in the stands, and, when they called the hurdles final, a great many people were clustered about the finish line, where the tape glimmered with ghostly promise for the winner. I ran in the next lane from the boy from Canton. We shook hands: a new friendship, a fierce rivalry, for I knew he would give no quarter, and I knew damn well that I wasn't planning to give any. We got down on the blocks. Before us was a green sea of grass with faint line stripes from spring practice across it. I concentrated on getting as much pressure on my legs as I could. I would try to get off well, though I was too big to hope for a really fast start. The gun cracked, and we were gone. I paid no attention to where anyone else was but concentrated on form and on picking up speed between the hurdles. But I could dimly sense the Canton boy. At the fifth hurdle I could tell that we were dead even. The finish-line crowd was coming at us like a hurricane. I concentrated on staying low over the hurdles and made really good moves on the next three. I began to edge him by inches, and by the next two hurdles I thought that if I didn't hit the next two I'd make it. I also said to myself, as I remember, don't play it safe. Go low over the last stick, and then give it everything you've got up the final straight.

Reading for Meaning

1 Locate the underlined words in the paragraph, and reread the sentences in which they appear. Write your own definiton of what the word means in that sentence. Use a dictionary if necessary.

"suited up" _____

clustered _____

glimmered _____

ghostly _____

rivalry _____

quarter _____

faint _____

cracked _____

dimly _____

edge _____

Reading for Structure

2 Is there a topic sentence in this paragraph? _____

3 What is the topic being developed?

_____

_____

4 What kind of chronological organization is used in this paragraph?

_____

5 List the transition words used. _____

6 Are any of the major ideas out of chronological order?

_____

7 What is the subject of the first three sentences?

_____ , _____ , _____

8 What is the general subject of sentences 4 to 9? _____

_____

9 What is the general subject of sentences 10 to 17? _____

_____

10 Are these three major divisions in chronological order? _____

11 What words tell the reader the points during the race at which each action occurs?

_____

_____

12 Transitions, repetition of important words such as *hurdle*, and the use of pronouns to link sentences help to unify paragraphs. In this paragraph, who is *he*?

_____

_____

9 Now read the entire essay "James Dickey's Glory" with the sample paragraph in place.

[1] In 1940 I was a senior in high school. My main sport was football, but my <u>preference</u> was really track. I was a big strong animal who could run fast, and I gloried in this fact. My conference, though I lived in Atlanta, was not the conference in which the big Atlanta high schools competed. I ran in the North Georgia Interscholastic Conference, or N.G.I.C., as it was popularly known. The high-hurdles event, which was my specialty, was often held on grass up the middle of a football field. This was the case at the 1940 N.G.I.C. meet. We qualified in the afternoon, all of us trying hard but not so hard as to tire ourselves out for the night's final. In the trials I lost to a fine hurdler from Canton, Georgia, and then went out with him, soaked with shower water, and got a cheeseburger. I felt that I had not run well, that my start had been bad, that I had not been able to get a good grip on the turf with my spikes, that I had been too high over the hurdles, that my finish had been poor. But my conqueror had set a new N.G.I.C. record and he should have.

[2] When I suited up for the finals, though, I was ready. I felt

that I had come to run. It was a cool night and there were several hundred people in the stands, and, when they called the hurdles final, a great many people were clustered about the finish line, where the tape glimmered with ghostly promise for the winner. I ran in the next lane from the boy from Canton. We shook hands: a new friendship, a fierce rivalry, for I knew he would give no quarter, and I knew damn well that I wasn't planning to give any. We got down on the blocks. Before us was a green sea of grass with faint line stripes from spring practice across it. I concentrated on getting as much pressure on my legs as I could. I would try to get off well, though I was too big to hope for a really fast start. The gun cracked, and we were gone. I paid no attention to where anyone else was but concentrated on form and on picking up speed between the hurdles. But I could dimly sense the Canton boy. At the fifth hurdle I could tell that we were dead even. The finish-line crowd was coming at us like a hurricane. I concentrated on staying low over the hurdles and made really good moves on the next three. I began to edge him by inches, and by the next two hurdles I thought that if I didn't hit the next two I'd make it. I also said to myself, as I remember, don't play it safe. Go low over the last stick, and then give it everything you've got up to the final straight.

[3] But I did hit the last hurdle. I hit it with the inner ankle of my left foot, tearing the flesh to the bone, as I found out later, and the injury left a scar which I bear to this day. However, my <u>frenzied</u> <u>momentum</u> was such that I won by a yard, <u>careening</u> wildly into the crowd after the tape broke around my neck. I smashed into the spectators and bowled over a little boy, hitting straight into his nose with my knee. He lay on the smoky grass crying, his nose bleeding, and I came back blowing like a wounded stallion, everybody congratulating me on a new N.G.I.C. record. But I went to the boy, raised him up in my arms, wiped the blood from his nose, tried to comfort him, and kissed him. That raising-up of an injured, unknown child was the greatest thing that I have ever <u>gleaned</u> from sports.

Reading for Meaning

1 Locate the underlined words in the essay, and reread the sentences in which they appear. Write your own definition of what the word means in that sentence. Use a dictionary if necessary.

preference _____

frenzied _____

momentum _____

careening _____

gleaned _____

Reading for Structure

2 Paragraph 1 begins with an introductory section and then ends with a chronological section. Where does the chronological organization start in paragraph 1?

_____

3 What transition words are used in paragraph 1? _____

4 What words show the relationship between paragraphs 1 and 2?

_____

5 What words show the relationship between paragraphs 2 and 3?

_____

6 What is the topic of paragraph 3?

_____

7 List the main supporting ideas in paragraph 3.

_____

_____

8 What order are these ideas in?

_____

9 List the transition words used in paragraph 3.

_____

10 Why aren't these chronological transition words?

_____

11 What sentence in the last paragraph describes the purpose of the essay?

_____

Comprehension Test

12 About how old was Dickey in 1940? _____

13 What was his *main* sport in high school? _____

14 What sport is the story about? Why? _____

_____

15 What event is Dickey's specialty? _____

16 What was the hometown of the boy who beat Dickey in the

trials? _____

17 At what point in the final race did Dickey overtake his opponent?

_____

18 What happened to Dickey at the last hurdle? _____

19 How many hurdles were there in the race? _____

20 What was Dickey thinking about immediately before the race?

_____

21 What was his initial strategy to win? _____

_____

22 What was his strategy at the end of the race?

_____

23   What happened *after* the last hurdle? _____

_____

24   What did Dickey do immediately after the race? _____

_____

25   At the end of the first paragraph, is Dickey making excuses for his poor performance in the trials? Why?

_____

_____

26   Why do you think Dickey concludes by saying, "That raising-up of an injured unknown child was the greatest thing that I have ever gleaned from sports"?

_____

_____

_____

27   Why does Dickey use the words *glimmered*, *ghostly*, and *a green sea of grass* to describe the scene of the race?

_____

_____

_____

Writing Assignments

28   Write a paragraph describing the most important thing you ever "gleaned" from sports.

_____

_____

_____

_____

_____

_____

_____

_____

_____

_____

_____

_____

_____

_____

_____

_____

_____

_____

_____

_____

_____

_____

_____

_____

_____

_____

_____

29 Write a paragraph describing the most important thing that has happened to you in the last two or three years.

_____

_____

Readings_____

Building Men the
Marine Corps Way

Harry Crews

10 The following two paragraphs are samples from the essay that begins on page 66. By reading these paragraphs and answering the questions, you will prepare yourself to read and understand the entire essay more easily.

Buddy may have gone crazy. But he may not have. He may have just been smarter than the rest of us. He had always read his Bible a lot. But after about three weeks, he started reading it all the time. He didn't ignore his work or anything, and his equipment was always in order and ready; but when he had a free minute, out would come the Bible. And he got quieter. Unless it was to try to help somebody who was hurt, he never spoke. He did seem to be in a little bit of a <u>daze</u>. But I saw him for weeks in the P.O.U. platoon and he would, if we were close enough and his D.I.'s were looking the other way, always give me some sign to let me know he saw me, too. So he may only have been <u>sly</u> and bright and mature beyond his years.

When they got ready to let one of the recruits out of P.O.U. platoon and send him home to his mother and father, they would take him over to the <u>base</u> barber and shave his head skin smooth again. Then they would dress him in civilian clothes nobody could imagine. I don't know what madman bought those clothes or where he got them, but it made us <u>shudder</u> when we saw one of us headed for the gate—sometimes walking backward—<u>clowned out</u> and shaven down.

Reading for Meaning

1 Locate the underlined words in the paragraphs and reread the sentences in which they appear. Write your own definition of what the word means in that sentence. Use a dictionary if necessary.

daze _____

sly _____

base _____

shudder _____

clowned out _____

Reading for Structure

2　What is the topic sentence of the first paragraph?

_____

3　List the main supporting ideas in the first paragraph. _____

_____

4　In what order are these ideas arranged? _____

5　List the transition words that signal this arrangement.

_____

6　What is the function of the last sentence in paragraph 1?

_____

_____

7　List the main supporting ideas in paragraph 2. _____

_____

8　In what order are these ideas arranged? _____

9 Are transition words used? List them. _____

_____

10 Is there a topic sentence in paragraph 2? _____

11 Now read the entire essay "Building Men the Marine Corps Way" with the sample paragraphs in place.

[1] The only reason I got through boot camp was Buddy. He got me through that first month before he went to the P.O.U. platoon and after the first month I was calmed down enough to make it the rest of the way by myself. When I was about to <u>come apart</u> out on the field, he used to talk to the back of my head. He marched right behind me in my squad and it seemed he could always tell if I was about to go down and if the drill instructor was far enough away he'd start talking to me.

[2] He was from Alabama and he had the softest, sweetest voice I'll ever hear. He'd tell me about places he'd swum as a boy, streams, running dogs at night, the sound of their baying voices, the way he and his daddy used to make coffee—called sawmill coffee—where the coffee grounds are dumped right into the water and set on an open fire.

[3] I was there when they took Buddy away. They took him to the P.O.U. platoon. P.O.U. stands for Psychological Observation Unit. I didn't get a chance to say good-bye to him. To thank him. Two military police came and got him one morning and took him. We were fairly accustomed to seeing somebody taken to the P.O.U. platoon. As I remember, we started with about sixty recruits in our platoon and I think about forty-five left the island in uniform. The rest either went out with things like busted ear-drums, or they went to the P.O.U. platoon for a while and then went home. Everybody was scared to death of being sent to the P.O.U. platoon. Better to leave with a broken arm, or a chewed-off thumb, than to leave through the P.O.U. platoon.

[4] What the United States Marines did was to make the Psychological Observation Unit walk backward in front of the mess hall while all the other platoons were standing there waiting to eat, or make the P.O.U. recruits crawl across the drill field, or bark like dogs in chorus. Their drill instructors usually didn't give ordinary commands either. To stop them the D.I.'s would give such <u>precise</u> commands as: "Whoa, herd!" To start them off was sometimes a simple "Giddyup!"

[5] You could go to the P.O.U. platoon because you walked funny, or because you didn't qualify at the rifle range with your M–1, or because a D.I. discovered, or decided, that you <u>lisped</u>, or—sometimes—because you went crazy. More people than you'd think simply went crazy. An <u>enormous</u> and beautifully muscled boy who had been a football player just before coming to Parris Island had some sort of total nervous collapse the second day we were there and couldn't talk. He could only cry and scream.

[6] Buddy may have gone crazy. But he may not have. He may have just been smarter than the rest of us. He had always read his Bible a lot. But after about three weeks, he started reading it all the time. He didn't ignore his work or anything, and his equipment was always in order and ready; but when he had a free minute, out would come the Bible. And he got quieter. Unless it was to try to help somebody who was hurt, he never spoke. He did seem to be in a little bit of a daze. But I saw him for weeks in the P.O.U. platoon and he would, if we were close enough and his D.I.'s were looking the other way, always give me some sign to let me know he saw me, too. So he may only have been sly and bright and mature beyond his years.

[7] When they got ready to let one of the recruits out of the P.O.U. platoon and send him home to his mother and father, they would take him over to the base barber and shave his head skin smooth again. Then they would dress him in civilian clothes nobody could imagine. I don't know what madman bought those clothes or where he got them, but it made us shudder when we saw one of us headed for the gate—sometimes walking backward—clowned out and shaven down.

[8] I saw Buddy by accident the day he left. We were out on the drill field down by the phony flag raising on Mount Suribachi on Iwo Jima when I saw him come out of a building and head for the gate. He had on yellow shoes that looked like maybe they were also patent leather, and green socks. You could see the green socks fine because his red pants were about four inches too short for him. An <u>electric</u> purple shirt was neatly tucked into the pants. His tie—a kind of off blue—was so long he should have tucked it in, too, but he hadn't; it hung low enough to cover his fly.

[9] He was a long way away and I watched him, only my eyes moving, my head rock still, standing at parade rest. Five yards from the gate, with nobody around to make him do it, he suddenly whipped around and started walking backward. He walked right on through the gate backward, and as he did the solid gold tooth he wore on the right side of his mouth caught and winked the sun directly at me.

Reading for Meaning

1 Locate the underlined words in the essay, and reread the sentences in which they appear. Write your own definition of what the word means in that sentence. Use a dictionary if necessary.

come apart _____

precise _____

lisped _____

enormous _____

electric _____

Reading for Structure

2 Is paragraph 3 organized chronologically? Why? _____

_____

3 Is paragraph 5 organized chronologically? Why? _____

_____

4 List the main supporting ideas in the last paragraph. _____

_____

_____

5 How are they arranged? _____

6 Is there a topic sentence for the last paragraph? Why? _____

_____

7 What is the topic of the last paragraph? _____

_____

8 The arrangements that can be used to organize paragraphs can also be used to organize essays. Even though some of the *paragraphs* in this essay do not use chronological organization, what organization is used to organize the *whole essay?*

_____

_____

9 List the topic of each paragraph in order.

_____

_____

_____

_____

_____

_____

_____

_____

Comprehension Test

10 Where was Buddy from? _____

11 How did Buddy help the narrator? _____

_____

12 What was the Psychological Observation Unit? _____

_____

13 Describe the scene when Buddy leaves for the P.O.U. _____

_____

_____

_____

_____

14 Why was the P.O.U. feared? _____

_____

15 What kinds of things could get a soldier transferred to the P.O.U.?

_____

_____

_____

_____

_____

_____

16 Why did Buddy end up in the P.O.U.? _____

_____

_____

17 In paragraph 6, can we tell if Buddy really has gone "crazy"?

_____

18 How did the P.O.U. dress recruits to send them home?

_____

_____

_____

_____

19 Describe the clothes the P.O.U. gave Buddy. _____

_____

_____

_____

_____

20 What does Buddy do at the very end of the essay? _____

_____

21 What does this tell the reader? _____

_____

22 Who is the main character of this essay? _____

23 Does Buddy tell the story? _____

24 Who *does* tell the story? _____

Writing Assignments

25 Write a paragraph that describes an incident in which a friend helped you.

_____

_____

_____

_____

_____

_____

_____

_____

_____

_____

_____

_____

_____

_____

_____

_____

26   Write a paragraph that explains what you do to escape either mentally or physically from situations that are unbearably boring or lonely.

_____

_____

_____

_____

_____

_____

_____

_____

_____

_____

_____

_____

_____

_____

_____

_____

_____

_____

_____

_____

_____

_____

_____

Readings _____

Twenty-six Hours of Insanity:
A Marijuana Nightmare

Robert C. Tucker

12 The following three paragraphs are samples from the essay that begins on page 80. Until now, you have been looking at individual paragraphs, but in any essay paragraphs do not exist individually. They grow out of one another and are linked in ways you should be able to discover. Now you will begin to see not only how an individual paragraph is arranged, but also how groups of paragraphs are arranged. Also, by reading these three paragraphs and answering the questions, you will prepare yourself to read and understand the entire essay more easily.

When we arrived in New York (at 9:30 P.M.), I sat down with a <u>martini</u> and relaxed for an hour. I then showered and dressed and left the apartment around 11:00 P.M. It took almost an hour to drive to the party. Once there, I had a scotch and drank a glass of wine. I noticed that many people were going in and out of a small <u>interior</u> room. I decided that this was the "<u>reefer</u>" <u>room</u> and moved toward it.

Once I was in the door, a <u>colleague</u> greeted me and handed me a very thin tightly rolled cigarette. I took several puffs and noticed that it was mild and burned very, very slowly. After I had finished that cigarette, I left the room feeling somewhat disappointed that I wasn't at least a little high. Before I had walked <u>approximately</u> 30 feet, however, I noticed that I was in fact high, unusually and unpleasantly high. I walked around a little bit, trying to <u>get myself together</u>. Fearing that my <u>aimless</u> pacing might appear <u>bizarre</u> to others, I decided to just stand in the doorway watching the partyers.

As I stood there I realized my head would not clear and, if anything, my condition was going to worsen. So, I decided to try to walk to the bathroom. Walking was an <u>ordeal</u>: My <u>gait</u> seemed odd, and I didn't want anyone who knew me to notice my staggering (if I was in fact staggering).

74

Reading for Meaning

1 Locate the underlined words in the paragraphs, and reread the sentences in which they appear. Write your own definition of what the word means in that sentence. Use a dictionary if necessary.

martini _____

interior _____

"reefer" room _____

colleague _____

approximately _____

get myself together _____

aimless _____

bizarre _____

ordeal _____

gait _____

Reading for Structure

2 Which is the topic sentence in the first paragraph? _____

_____

3 List the major supporting ideas in the first paragraph. _____

_____

_____

4 List the transitions that indicate the relationships between these ideas.

_____

_____

75

5 What sort of arrangement is used in this paragraph? _____

6 What transition phrase signals a relationship between the subject of paragraph 1 and the events narrated in paragraph 2?

7 Is there a topic sentence in paragraph 2? _____

8 List the *chronological* transitions in paragraph 2. _____

9 Is there a transition in paragraph 2 that is not a chronological transition? Why? _____

10 Which words in paragraph 3 signal a relationship between the subject of paragraph 2 and paragraph 3?

13 Now read these three paragraphs that have also been selected from the essay that begins on page 80. Reading these paragraphs and answering the questions following them will help you to understand the entire essay.

When we arrived at the hospital I explained my condition to a nurse, <u>withholding</u> the fact that I had smoked a <u>joint</u>. I calmly gave information such as my name, address, telephone number, Social Security number, date of birth, nearest relative, etc. It took her a while to appreciate that I was in a <u>psychotic</u>-like state, but she seemed to be <u>sympathetic</u>. Then, a man in a white coat explained that I would have to go to another hospital. I tried to tell him that since time was not passing for me, I might not make it to the other hospital and that I needed <u>medication</u>, such as Thorazine, Valium, or meprobamate. My protest was to no <u>avail</u>, however. He simply repeated his original statement. It then occurred to me that time spent arguing with him could best be used getting to another hospital, so I asked if he could get Roy for me. He shook his head, but walked out and told Roy where to take me.

As we pulled into the hospital, the car was <u>vibrating</u>, and I heard air <u>whiz</u> past, but we seemed to be <u>suspended</u> in space. My sense of motion was <u>intact</u>, but my sense of forward movement was totally absent.

When we pulled into the hospital driveway, I was astonished because I really hadn't thought we would get there. Before going in the doors, I asked Roy to be my spokesman because I had no confidence in my ability to communicate. We entered, and I sat in the sitting room while Roy explained to a nurse that I needed to see a doctor.

Reading for Meaning

1 Locate the underlined words in the paragraph, and reread the sentences in which they appear. Write your own definition of what the word means in that sentence. Use a dictionary if necessary.

withholding _____

joint _____

psychotic _____

sympathetic _____

medication _____

avail _____

vibrating _____

whiz _____

suspended _____

intact _____

Reading for Structure

2 What events are the subject of paragraph 1? _____

_____

3 Which is the topic sentence in paragraph 1? _____

_____

4 List the transitions used in paragraph 1. _____

_____

5 What is the arrangement of the main supporting ideas in paragraph 1?

_____

_____

6 What is the subject of paragraph 2? _____

_____

7 What function does the phrase *As we pulled into the hospital* perform?

_____

_____

_____

8 List the chronological transition words and phrases used in paragraph 3.

_____

_____

_____

_____

4 Now, read these two paragraphs from the essay beginning on page 80, and answer the questions following them. This will aid you in understanding the entire essay.

Alert and intense, I completed the 45-minute drive to my brother-in-law's house. Everything was quite smooth until I began to circle the block where his apartment was located. As I proceeded down the street, I noticed a parked police car. I knew I was doing something wrong. As I turned the corner I heard the police siren. I said to myself, "Oh, s—t! I've gotten this far and now I screw up." I considered trying to outrun the cops, then pulled over and stepped out of the car. The police parked behind me with their lights flashing and jumped out.

They asked me for my license and registration and then told me I had gone down a one-way street the wrong way. I calmly apologized and, since I was clearly an out-of-towner and appeared to be sober and respectable, they told me to be careful and let me go.

Reading for Meaning

1 Locate the underlined words in the paragraphs, and reread the sentences in which they appear. Write your own definition of what the word means in that sentence. Use a dictionary if necessary.

alert _____

intense _____

out-of-towner _____

sober _____

respectable _____

Reading for Structure

2 What is the subject of these two paragraphs? _____

_____

3 Is there a topic sentence? _____

4 List the transitions used in these two paragraphs. _____

_____

_____

5 Why is this selection separated into two paragraphs? _____

_____

6 Why are the paragraphs separated at the eighth sentence?

_____

_____

15 Now read the entire essay "Twenty-six Hours of Insanity" with the sample paragraphs in place.

[1] With "the great grass debates" sure to attract <u>media</u> and voter attention over the months to come, this carefully observed and professionally analyzed marijuana "bad trip" provides <u>grist</u> for those who argue that the existing laws ought to be retained or even toughened.

[2] Background: The narrator, whom we refer to as Dr. Smith, is a 35-year-old male clinical psychologist. He is married, has three children, and resides in the suburbs of New Haven, Connecticut. <u>Prior</u> to the experience we will be describing, he had smoked marijuana only ten to fifteen times.

[3] Dr. Smith's narrative: I had been invited to a Friday-evening party in the Bronx. My wife decided to visit her brother in lower Manhattan while I attended the party. We planned to spend the night at her brother's house and return home the next evening.

[4] When we arrived in New York (at 9:30 P.M.), I sat down with a martini and relaxed for an hour. I then showered and dressed and left the apartment around 11 P.M. It took almost an hour to drive to the party. Once there, I had a scotch and drank a glass of wine. I noticed that many people were going in and out of a small interior room. I decided that this was the "reefer" room and moved toward it.

[5] Once I was in the door, a colleague greeted me and handed me a very thin tightly rolled cigarette. I took several puffs and noticed that it was mild and burned very, very slowly. After I had finished that cigarette, I left the room feeling somewhat disappointed that I wasn't at least a little high. Before I had walked approximately 30 feet, however, I noticed that I was in fact high, unusually and unpleasantly high. I walked around a little bit, trying to get myself together. Fearing that my aimless pacing might appear bizarre to others, I decided to just stand in the doorway watching the partyers.

[6] As I stood there I realized my head would not clear and, if anything, my condition was going to worsen. So, I decided to try to walk to the bathroom. Walking was an ordeal: My gait seemed odd, and I didn't want anyone who knew me to notice my staggering (if I was in fact staggering).

[7] Finally I reached the bathroom but found that there was a line to get in. I was disappointed but remained calm. I felt that once I was in the bathroom I would be able to relax and get better control over the situation.

[8] Suddenly, I noticed that I was next in line for the bathroom. It was as if I had somehow lost a period of minutes. As I was standing there, a casually dressed young man came up to me and asked, "Is this the line for the bathroom?" I nodded affirmatively. He paused a second, then knocked on the door. Strangely enough, the man who was already in the bathroom let him in.

[9] This puzzled me. I figured they had to be a new breed of homosexual, or heroin addicts. While I was thinking about what had happened, a woman approached me; I don't remember our conversation, but I do remember seeing a large crowd of people in the hallway. The two men were in the bathroom

for a long time, and I felt a little shaky. I was getting higher and higher.

[10] Suddenly I turned around and realized that there were only two people in the hall—myself and a woman behind me. It occurred to me that I was hallucinating, that the two men were not really in the bathroom together, and that the friendly woman and the crowd had never really been there . . . that I had been alone in the hall all the time. Then, after an <u>interminably</u> long time during which my head swirled uncontrollably, the bathroom door opened and two men calmly walked out. "I'll be damned," I thought, "I really saw what I saw!"

[11] I walked into the bathroom and tried to relax, but I felt no better. I knew I could not stay in the bathroom very long, so I left and sat on the floor in another room. There I decided that I was suffering under the affects of some powerful drug whose name, nature, and <u>potency</u> were unknown to me.

[12] I was fearful of the <u>consequences</u> of my <u>predicament</u>. I wondered whether there <u>would be</u> long-term psychological problems, and was greatly concerned about how this situation would affect my family, my reputation, and my career. BIG TIME PROFESSOR FREAKS OUT ON DRUGS read the headline that flashed through my swirling head. I was crazy, and I was terrified.

[13] I knew I needed help, so I sought out my friend Roy, the only person at the party I felt I could trust.

[14] When I found him I explained that I was experiencing some drug-related difficulty, and we left the party.

[15] As we walked out, we passed Roy's car, and I noticed that there was a man in it who seemed to be experiencing difficulty similar to my own. I decided that I would sit in Roy's car.

[16] Roy attempted to comfort me, but I felt guilty about keeping him away from the party and knew that I needed to sleep, so I suggested that he return to the party. He agreed after I assured him I would be all right.

[17] Sleep was not <u>forthcoming</u>, however; I had a feeling that I was slowly losing control of myself and that if I let go, I would go crazy or die.

[18] During this period, time passed in an extraordinarily slow fashion. I found that each second was <u>equivalent</u> to several hours. I reminded myself that I was high and that I would eventually be relieved of this situation, but I calculated that it would take the equivalent of hundreds of years for relief to come.

[19] I considered the notion of hell, and it occurred to me that this was what hell would be like for me—a <u>disembodied</u> <u>intelligence</u> painfully floating through <u>ethereal</u> nothingness. Alone, with no <u>reference</u> points in time or space—eternally locked into an <u>existential dilemma</u>. Totally without hope.

[20] This consideration put me in touch with the solution to this crisis: I had to get to a hospital where I could receive medication to relieve that symptom which prevented the passage of time. It occurred to me that the only way to do this would be to get Roy. I didn't feel, however, that I could go back up to the party by myself.

[21] Finally, I asked the man in the front seat if he could get Roy for me. His response was, "Man, I'm in bad shape too." It then occurred to me that all I had to do was stand up and begin walking. After I returned to the party, I told Roy that I needed to get to the hospital. He agreed to take me.

[22] When we arrived at the hospital I explained my condition to a nurse, withholding the fact that I smoked a joint. I calmly gave information such as my name, address, telephone number, Social Security number, date of birth, nearest relative, etc. It took her a while to appreciate that I was in a psychotic-like state, but she seemed to be sympathetic. Then, a man in a white coat explained that I would have to go to another hospital. I tried to tell him that since time was not passing for me, I might not make it to the other hospital and that I needed medication, such as Thorazine, Valium, or meprobamate. My protest was to no avail, however. He simply repeated his original statement. It then occurred to me that time spent arguing with him could best be used getting to another hospital, so I asked if he would get Roy for me. He shook his head, but walked out and told Roy where to take me.

[23] As we drove to the hospital, the car was vibrating, and I heard air whiz past, but we seemed to be suspended in space. My sense of motion was intact, but my sense of forward movement was totally absent.

[24] When we pulled into the hospital driveway, I was astonished because I really hadn't thought we would get there. Before going in the doors, I asked Roy to be my spokesman because I had no confidence in my ability to communicate. We entered, and I sat in the sitting room while Roy explained to a nurse that I needed to see a doctor.

[25] Finally, a female psychiatrist appeared and led Roy and me into what seemed to be a mental-health center connected to the general hospital. As we walked I noted mangled bodies and injured people in all rooms that we passed. At last we reached an office in the deserted mental-health center and proceeded with the interview.

[26] I described what was happening to me in a quite <u>coherent</u> and orderly way. I then said that I knew exactly what I needed, but before I could get it out, I forgot what I needed. Then I recovered and told her that I needed Valium or meprobamate (I had decided that Thorazine would be too powerful). To my surprise, she agreed with me and elected to prescribe Valium.

[27] I was impressed by her cooperation and felt a swell of good feeling for her. I thanked her and walked toward the pharmacy. We arrived there at approximately 4:00 A.M. but found that it would not open until 4:30 A.M. This was a disaster, since I wasn't sure that I could last until then.

[28] As I was wondering what I should do, a funny feeling descended form the top of my head down to my crotch. My head cleared <u>perceptibly</u> and I experienced a moderate <u>euphoria</u> for a few seconds. I was sure I was coming down; my time sense was less <u>distorted</u> and my motor control was excellent. Relieved and somewhat cocky, I suggested that we leave without filling the prescription. I felt that if I could get back to the party, my mind would clear enough in another hour or so to permit me to drive back to Manhattan, so we returned to Roy's car.

[29] As we drove, I noted that even though things had improved <u>dramatically</u> I was still in very bad shape.

[30] Back at the party I felt uncomfortable <u>mingling</u> with the few remaining people. I wasn't sure whether I could drive back to lower Manhattan or not, but I decided that I should try.

[31] I walked out of the house unassisted and found my way to my car. I was distressed by the <u>realization</u> that I was higher than I had originally believed, but relieved when I discovered that I could drive without weaving.

[32] Unfortunately, after making the first two turns, I got lost. It was after 4:30 A.M.; there were no people out, and most gas stations were closed. Becoming more and more fearful, I decided to drive down a major <u>thoroughfare</u>. When I stopped at a light, I rolled down my window and asked a man for directions.

[33] More by luck than by skill, I followed his instructions correctly and ended up on the appropriate street. Once on the road, driving was not very difficult, but I was easily <u>distracted</u> and I feared I would veer off the road or go through a red light.

[34] Alert and <u>intense</u>, I completed the 45-minute drive to

my brother-in-law's house. Everything was quite smooth until I began to circle the block where his apartment was located. As I proceeded down the street, I noticed a parked police car. I knew I was doing something wrong. As I turned the corner I heard the police siren. I said to myself, "Oh, s—t! I've gotten this far and now I screw up." I considered trying to out run the cops, then pulled over and stepped out of the car. The police parked behind me with their lights flashing and jumped out.

[35] They asked for my license and registration and then told me I had gone down a one-way street the wrong way. I calmly apologized and, since I was clearly an out-of-towner and appeared to be sober and respectable, they told me to be careful and let me go.

[36] Greatly relieved, I slowly and carefully drove the last two blocks to the apartment. My entrance into the apartment was so noiseless that no one woke up. I went to the bathroom, brushed my teeth, and slid into bed.

[37] My expectation of relief once I was in bed was unfulfilled. My head still swirled and I couldn't relax. I was still miserable. I remained in bed until about 11:30 A.M. trying to sleep, but to no avail. My mind was swirling and time was still passing slowly.

[38] During that day I ate very little, had no appetite, and had no interest in food or drink. I couldn't concentrate well enough to watch TV or listen to music, and I was uncomfortable whether I was sitting, standing, or reclining.

[39] When we left New York that afternoon I decided to drive, thinking that time might pass a little more quickly if I were occupied.

[40] On the highway I was extremely careful and concerned myself with making it from one toll station to the next. When we finally pulled off the highway at home, I felt immensely proud of my achievement.

[41] It was about seventeen hours after I had taken the drug, and I was still high; I was also constantly on guard, because I feared I might ramble in conversation or stumble as I was walking (my wife assured me that I appeared to be quite normal, however). That night, finally, after twenty-six hours of torment, I feel asleep.

[42] When I woke up Sunday morning I noted that I had slept for at least five hours and felt much better. I remembered my dreams and was fascinated by the fact that they were all drug-related and/or psychedelic in nature—rich with drug symbolism.

[43] Throughout the day I felt very energetic and my appe-

tite returned. I read the papers, watched T.V., listened to music, and talked with my family.

[44] When I went to bed that night I was strangely <u>apprehensive</u>. I was highly sensitive to sounds and experienced mild <u>anxiety</u> in response to normal house and wind sounds. I had <u>difficulty</u> falling asleep and slept fitfully.

[45] I was quite tired the next day, but was convinced that the drug effects had run their course. I then began to assemble the little notes I had compiled during all except the peak period of my <u>intoxication</u>. I jotted down further notes, relaxed, reflected, and celebrated my return to life.

Reading for Meaning

1 Locate the underlined words in the essay, and reread the sentences in which they appear. Write your own definition of what the word means in that sentence. Use a dictionary if necessary.

media _____

grist _____

prior _____

affirmatively _____

interminably _____

potency _____

consequences _____

predicament _____

forthcoming _____

equivalent _____

disembodied intelligence _____

ethereal _____

reference _____

existential dilemma _____

coherent _____

The words in the left-hand column are underlined in the essay. Reread the sentences in which they appear, and pick, from the choices at the right, the word that is closest in meaning. Circle your answer.

perceptibly	slightly	noticeably	evenly
euphoria	elation	unawareness	depression
distorted	realistic	perverted	irregular
dramatically	considerably	vividly	theatrically
mingling	blending	avoiding	interacting
realization	completion	awareness	attainment
thoroughfare	private drive	large street	lane
distracted	diverted	deviated	amused
intense	calm	violent	strongly con-centrating
unfulfilled	satisfied	disappointed	incompleted
immensely	extremely	huge	infinitely
symbolism	representations	dreams	sensuality
apprehensive	anxious	captive	comprehen-sive
anxiety	pain	fear	uneasiness
intoxication	drugged stupor	poisoned	frenzied

Reading for Structure

2 The supporting ideas in the paragraphs you have read are all arranged chronologically; how are the *paragraphs* arranged?

_____

3 Are there any exceptions? _____

Comprehension Test

4 Place the following sentences in chronological order by numbering them in order in the blanks beside each phrase:

_____ A. Smith discovers the "reefer" room.
_____ B. Smith gets stopped by the police.
_____ C. Smith goes to the hospital.
_____ D. Smith can't sleep at his brother-in-law's house.
_____ E. Smith wakes up and writes down his notes.
_____ F. Smith drinks a scotch and a martini.
_____ G. Smith drives to his brother-in-law's house.
_____ H. Smith lies down in the car.

5 List the events that lead up to Dr. Smith's trip to New York.

_____

_____

_____

_____

_____

_____

_____

_____

_____

_____

6 What does Smith do to "get ready" for the party?

_____

_____

7 Why would there be a *separate* room at the party for smoking "reefers"?

_____

8 What is the first effect of the marijuana on Smith?

_____

_____

9 Why is he so worried about the possibility that he is staggering?

_____

_____

10 Why does Smith find it strange that the man already occupying the bathroom admits someone before him? What does he assume?

_____

11 Standing outside the bathroom, Smith decides that he is hallucinating. Why?

_____

_____

12 Where does Smith decide to go immediately after leaving the bathroom?

_____

13 What is Smith's profession? _____

14 Why does this make him nervous? _____

_____

15 Whom does Smith turn to for help? _____

16 What does Roy do at first? _____

_____

17 What does Smith think about while he lies in the car near the party?

_____

_____

_____

18 After Smith leaves the car, where does he decide he needs to go?

_____

19 Describe the events of the visit to the first hospital. _____

_____

_____

_____

_____

_____

_____

20 What kind of hospital does the doctor send him to? Why?

_____

_____

21 Why does Smith keep insisting he needs Thorazine or Valium?

_____

_____

22 Finally, Smith gets his prescription; then he fails to wait to have it filled. Why?

_____

23 What effect does his "high" have on Smith's driving? _____

_____

24 What frightening thing happens on Smith's drive back to his brother-in-law's house?

_____

_____

_____

_____

25 When does the drug effect finally wear off? _____

26 What are Smith's feelings *after* his experience? _____

_____

_____

27 Why do you think he has taken notes during his experience?

_____

_____

Writing Assignments

28 Write a paragraph narrating your first encounter with the law.

_____

_____

_____

_____

_____

_____

29   Finish this sentence, and use it as the topic sentence of a chronologically organized paragraph:

"If I'd known it was going to be that kind of party, _____

_____

_____

_____

_____

_____

_____

_____

_____

_____

_____

_____

_____

_____

_____

_____

_____

_____

_____

30 Write a paragraph that describes a situation you were involved in but probably shouldn't have been.

_____

_____

_____

_____

_____

_____

_____

_____

_____

_____

_____

_____

_____

_____

_____

_____

_____

_____

_____

_____

Readings ————————

Mollie Moon

Stephen Birmingham

16 The following paragraph is a sample from the essay that begins on page 95. By reading this paragraph and answering the questions, you will prepare yourself to read and understand the entire essay more easily.

Mollie Moon was born in Hattiesburg, Mississippi, but "escaped at the age of nine months—<u>obviously</u> not under my own steam." The person who <u>engineered</u> her escape was her mother, an <u>energetic</u> lady who brought her to Cleveland and who for years was active in Republican politics there—remaining a Republican long after most blacks <u>transferred</u> their <u>allegiance</u> to the Democrats under Roosevelt. Mollie Moon was educated at Rusk University and at McHarry Medical Schools, where she earned a degree as a registered <u>pharmacist</u>, a profession she has never practiced. She also studied at Columbia and took courses in German and biology at the University of Berlin. Mollie Moon, clearly a woman of the world, says, "If you ask me, the main difference between upper-class Negroes and upper-class whites is that the Negroes are better educated." In travels that took her into the <u>segregated</u> South, she was <u>undaunted</u> by <u>discriminatory</u> regulations. "I just put on a <u>sari</u>, painted a red dot on my forehead, and said I was an Indian."

Reading for Meaning

1 Locate the underlined words in the paragraph, and reread the sentences in which they appear. Write your own definition of what the word means in that sentence. Use a dictionary if necessary.

obviously _____

engineered _____

energetic _____

transferred _____

allegiance _____

pharmacist _____

segregated _____

undaunted _____

discriminatory _____

sari _____

Reading for Structure

2 Is there a topic sentence? _____

3 List the main supporting ideas. _____

_____

_____

4 Insert the following transitions in appropriate places: *As a young woman, later,* and *after receiving my diploma.*

5 What kind of arrangement does this paragraph illustrate?

_____

_____

_____

7 Now read the entire essay "Mollie Moon" with the sample paragraph in place.

    [1] In recent years, of course, a number of <u>affluent</u> black families have moved out of Harlem—among them, the lady who is probably New York's leading black society woman, Mrs. Henry Lee Moon. Plump, fair-skinned, <u>animated</u>, with a <u>flair</u>

for startling and <u>exotic</u> clothes and jewelry, Mollie Moon is certainly one of New York's more colorful ladies. In her pretty apartment in Queens—the Moons moved out of Sugar Hill several years ago in <u>quest</u> of more space and cleaner air—Mollie Moon arranges herself against a large bouquet of gladioli and sips champagne. A <u>program</u> from the Bolshoi Ballet sits on her coffee table, and it is not one of the free-handout variety but the kind you pay for. It is clear that Mollie Moon is a woman of taste and <u>consequence</u>, and that her <u>status symbols</u> are the same as any white woman's in her station.

[2] Mollie Moon has been much photographed by the press and has a huge stack of eight-by-ten glossy prints to prove it. She has been photographed being <u>bussed</u> by former Mayor John V. Lindsay, chatting with the late Mrs. Robert Wagner, with Marietta Tree, Marian Anderson, Ralph Bunche, Lena Horne, Sammy Davis, Jr., Jeanne Murray Vanderbilt, the late Winthrop Rockefeller, Robert David Lion Gardiner (sixteenth lord of the manor of Gardiners Island), and Pope Pius XII (with whom Mollie Moon, a Catholic, had a <u>private audience</u>)—all of whom she counts among her many friends. Mollie Moon adores champagne, and it matches her <u>effervescent</u> personality. She never used to drink wine. Once, on an ocean voyage to Europe, she said to a steward in the dining room, "No wine for me, thank you." A friend turned to her in amazement and said, "Mollie, are you turning down champagne?" She cried, "Was that champagne?" She tried some, liked it, and has been sipping it ever since.

[3] Mollie Moon was born in Hattiesburg, Mississippi, but "escaped at the age of nine months—obviously not under my own steam." The person who engineered her escape was her mother, an energetic lady who brought her to Cleveland and who for years was active in Republican politics there—remaining a Republican long after most blacks transferred their allegiance to the Democrats under Roosevelt. Mollie Moon was educated at Rusk University and at McHarry Medical Schools, where she earned a degree as a registered pharmacist, a profession she has never practiced. She also studied at Columbia and took courses in German and biology at the University of Berlin. Mollie Moon, clearly a woman of the world, says, "If you ask me, the main difference between upper-class Negroes and upper-class whites is that the Negroes are better educated." On travels that took her into the segregated South, she was undaunted by discriminatory regulations. "I just put on a sari, painted a red dot on my forehead, and said I was an Indian."

[4] Back in Cleveland, she met her husband, an <u>erudite</u> man

who is a graduate of Ohio State School of Journalism and who wrote, briefly, for the *New York Times*—where old Mr. Sulzberger refused to give him a press card, saying that the *Times* was "not ready for that"—and later for the *Amsterdam News.* Henry Moon is now retired and is known, according to his wife, as "the best martini-maker on the East Coast." In New York, where the Moons have lived for the last 35 years, Mollie Moon threw herself into good works, and her name has decorated any number of boards and committees. At the moment, she is on the board of the Advisory Drug Committee, which reports to the commissioner of food and drugs in Washington. But her main philanthropic endeavor has been on behalf of the National Urban League, and for years she has been chairman of the Urban League Guild.

[5] In New York, Mollie Moon is known as "the black Perle Mesta." She is also known as the "Queen of the Cocktails-Five-to-Nine-Set." She loves parties, and there has been quite literally no one of importance in New York in the last three and a half decades who has not been to one of her entertainments. In her apartment, the telephone never stops ringing with party invitations. Her favorite party guest was Dr. Bunche, who also loved parties. "Oh, how that man loved parties!" she says. "Even when he was old and ill and losing his eyesight, he'd drop everything to go to a party. He'd come to my house for cocktails at five and stay until two in the morning."

[6] Mollie Moon's most celebrated annual party is New York's Beaux Arts Ball, which she inaugurated in 1942 on behalf of the Urban League and which has been a New York society feature ever since. Mollie Moon is considered a genius at getting leading white socialites to dress up and sit down at a dinner with celebrities from the black world of society, sports, and entertainment. One might not think that Josephine Baker and Marian Anderson would both turn up as honored guests at the same party, but Mollie Moon did it. And when Josephine Baker met Marian Anderson, Mme. Baker performed a deep curtsy. The Beaux Arts Ball used to be held in the old Savoy Hotel in Harlem—"in the days when Harlem was safe and gay and fun to go to"—but in recent years it has been held in the Waldorf-Astoria, always in February, "to relieve the midwinter doldrums." Though 1975 and 1976, because of the recession, were not banner years for the Beaux Arts Ball, its profits usually yield the Urban League about $20,000 annually and, over the years, it has netted the league over a half million dollars.

[7] The Beaux Arts Ball is famous for the dazzling spectacle of the costumes people turn up in and, at every ball, the most

97

spectacularly dressed person of all is its chairman. She appears in glittering headpieces of towering tinsel, furs, feathers, jewels, and gowns bedizened with sequins and gold pailletes. At a recent ball, the glamorous chairman was presented to the audience stepping out of a huge mock-up of a champagne bottle, wearing a gown of silver lamé, a jeweled breastplate and a crown of white ostrich plumes.

[8] Some black New Yorkers criticize Mollie Moon and call her a social butterfly. But she has her serious side. Not long ago, for example, she attended an Urban League conference in Atlanta, and a <u>diversion</u> offered to the conferees was a tour of the homes of the many wealthy blacks in the city. Mollie Moon <u>demurred</u>. "Why should I be interested in going to see the homes of wealthy blacks?" she says. "I said no. I told them I'd rather go to the museums or visit some of the local historical sights." She is aware that she has critics but pays them little heed. Probing through her huge collection of glossy photographs of herself and her famous friends, of her many public appearances in her extraordinary costumes, she says, "My only regret is that I'm not a size 12 anymore."

Reading for Meaning

1 Locate the underlined words in the essay, and reread the sentences in which they appear. Write your own definition of what the word means in that sentence. Use a dictionary if necessary.

affluent _____

animated _____

flair _____

exotic _____

quest _____

program _____

consequence _____

status symbols _____

bussed _____

private audience _____

effervescent _____

erudite _____

philanthropic _____

endeavor _____

literally _____

The words in the left-hand column are underlined in the essay. Reread the sentences in which they appear, and pick, from the choices at the right, the word that is closest in meaning. Circle your answer.

inaugurated	began	installed	elected
doldrums	parts of the ocean	listlessness	stagnation
recession	interruption	financial setback	withdrawal
diversion	pleasant pastime	deviation	misdirection
demurred	hesitated	objected	agreed

Reading for Structure

2 What is the subject of paragraph 1? _____

3 What is the subject of paragraph 2? _____

4 Do these paragraphs use chronological arrangement? _____

5 What is the subject of paragraph 4? _____

6 What is the subject of paragraph 5? _____

7 Which is the topic sentence of paragraph 5? _____

8 List the main supporting ideas in paragraph 5. Are they arranged chronologically?

_____

_____

_____

_____

_____

9 Why is the subject of paragraph 3 included before the subject of paragraph 4?

_____

10 What sort of relationship is there between the subjects of paragraphs 3, 4, and 5?

_____

_____

_____

_____

_____

11 Which is the topic sentence in paragraph 6? _____

_____

12 What details are used to support this topic sentence?

_____

_____

_____

_____

_____

13 What sort of arrangement is used to order these details?

_____

_____

14 Is paragraph 7 chronologically organized? _____

Comprehension Test

15 Describe Mollie Moon.

_____

_____

_____

_____

_____

_____

16 Where does Ms. Moon live? _____

17 Describe the setting (surroundings) of the interview.

_____

_____

_____

_____

_____

_____

_____

_____

_____

_____

18 Name five celebrities that Ms. Moon counts among her friends.

_____, _____, _____, _____,

_____.

19 Mollie Moon began drinking champagne in a fairly humorous way. Relate the story in your own words.

_____

_____

_____

_____

_____

_____

_____

_____

20 Where was Ms. Moon born? _____

21 Where did Ms. Moon move to from Mississippi? _____

22 Where was she educated? In what profession?

_____

23 What did Ms. Moon pose as on her journeys into the South?

_____

24 According to Ms. Moon, what is the main difference between upper-class blacks and upper-class whites?

_____

25 What was Ms. Moon's husband's profession at the time of their marriage?

_____

26 What three philanthropic organizations is Ms. Moon associated with?

_____, _____,

_____

27 Which of these may be considered her "main philanthropic endeavor"?

_____

28 What two nicknames does Ms. Moon go by?

_____, _____

29 What is Ms. Moon's most celebrated annual party?

_____

30 Where was this party traditionally held? Why was it moved to the Waldorf-Astoria?

_____, _____

31 Describe Mollie Moon's customary attire at her annual New York's Beaux Arts Ball.

_____

_____

_____

_____

32 What is the major accusation against Ms. Moon by her critics?

_____

33 At the end of the essay Mollie reflects on her life and has only one regret. What is it?

_____

34 Why do you think the author chose to include this comment?

_____

_____

_____

_____

_____

_____

_____

_____

_____

_____

_____

_____

_____

_____

Writing Assignment

35 In a paragraph, describe someone you consider successful. What has this person done that makes you think the person is a success?

_____

_____

_____

_____

_____

_____

_____

_____

_____

_____

_____

_____

_____

_____

_____

_____

_____

_____

_____

_____

_____

_____

Description:
3 Spatial Arrangement of Detail

In the last chapter you learned about the structure of paragraphs that describe events, things that can be organized and arranged according to chronology. This chapter will teach you the structure of paragraphs that are about people or objects—things that can be organized spatially, or according to their structure in space and location in space.

A descriptive paragraph will consist of supporting ideas that are specific details about the subject of the paragraph. The details develop, explain, or prove the topic sentence of the paragraph. There is no one absolutely correct way to arrange details for every descriptive paragraph. Each subject has its own structure, or the way it is organized, and a paragraph written about it should have an arrangement that will make the appearance of the subject clear to the reader. Describe a subject as you see it or imagine it.

The writer uses transitions that show the reader the arrangement of the subject; the reader must be aware of these transitions and follow the arrangement of the supporting ideas closely. Some of the transition words that indicate spatial arrangement of detail are *inside, outside, on top of this, to the left, to the right, near, next to this, at its side, to the north, farther down,* and so on. The list is probably endless.

If you are writing a descriptive paragraph and feel at a loss for an arrangement of detail, *climactic order* is a good order to follow. Most writers choose the arrangement that will present the reader with the most important or most interesting details last, so that the reader will remember these details longer. For example, there are many ways in which a description of this classroom might be arranged, but your perception of the room or your purpose in writing, combined with the principle of climactic order, would help you choose. A student who wanted to emphasize his or her own presence in the back of the classroom might describe the front of the room first, then the other students, then himself. A teacher would probably arrange the details in just the opposite order, to emphasize the teacher's own location at the front of the room; a lighting engineer would probably arrange the paragraph so that he could write about the inadequate lighting last; and someone in love with a student in the row farthest left would describe the room from right to left, so as to be able to write about the lover last. But the writer's task is always to give the reader as much help as possible so he can follow the arrangement; the writer does this by using transitions, by using words that indicate spatial relationships, and by repeating important words and phrases.

1 Read this sample paragraph, following its organization very closely by underlining transitions and numbering each supporting idea.

My favorite food is strawberry shortcake. I love the two-inch layer of thick, moist cake, with juicy red strawberries piled high on top of it, with the sweet strawberry juice flowing down over the cake. But what really finishes shortcake off for me is a topping of thick, white, fluffy whipped cream. I love to make myself a piece of shortcake and eat it slowly while I watch television or study.

1 Which sentence is the topic sentence? _____

2 Which sentence is the concluding sentence? _____

3 List the details that describe the shortcake. _____

_____

4 List the words and phrases that show the locations of each detail.

_____

_____

107

2 Read the following paragraph carefully.

My favorite snack food is pizza. I love it with beer or as a snack by itself. I like my pizza with very thick crust, covered with heaps of tomato sauce and huge amounts of rich cheese melted over the sauce. The minor little goodies such as mushrooms, peppers, onions, and pepperoni circles are sprinkled over the whole top of the pizza. I love good, homemade pizza because it hits the spot.

1 Which sentence is the topic sentence? _____

2 Which is the concluding sentence? _____

3 How is the supporting descriptive detail arranged? _____

_____

4 List the transitions or spatial words and phrases that signal this

arrangement. _____

3 Read the following paragraph, paying close attention to the arrangement of descriptive detail.

My favorite munchie is a cheeseburger. I prefer sesame seed buns on the outside that are fresh and soft. Between these is a delicious piece of cheese melted down over a well-seasoned beef patty. Finally, the cheese is carefully and completely covered with pickles, catsup, and mustard. These ingredients make cheeseburgers my favorite snack.

1 Which is the topic sentence? _____

2 Which is the concluding sentence? _____

3 How is the descriptive detail arranged? _____

4 List the transitions that signal this arrangement. _____

_____

5 Which detail is apparently most important to the author? How do you know?

_____

_____

_____

4 Read this paragraph carefully; pay close attention to transitions and supporting details.

My favorite food is pizza, and I usually buy it at a store near my home, at which they sell thick or thin crust pizzas, either large, medium, or small. They offer many different types of ingredients, such as sausages, extra cheese, hot peppers, onions, and many other spices. When I go there, I usually order a small, thick pizza with extra sausage.

1 Is this a descriptive paragraph? Why? _____

_____

5 Read the following paragraph, paying close attention to the arrangement of descriptive detail. Underline the transitions.

I would someday like to live in a split-level home with three levels. I would like the outside to be light brown brick, with tan shutters and trim. On the first level, I want a game room and large swimming pool. On the second level, I plan to have a kitchen, den, living room, and a breakfast room. On the third level I would like four bedrooms with one huge master bedroom containing a fountain. I plan two baths on each level. At the side of the master bedroom I would like a mirrored dressing room with a chandelier. Off the den, I plan to have a large family room with an open fireplace and sliding glass windows leading to a redwood deck.

1 Which is the topic sentence? _____

2 How is the descriptive detail arranged? _____

_____

3 What transitions signal this arrangement? _____

_____

4 How is the detail that describes the third level arranged?

_____

5 What transitions emphasize this arrangement? _____

_____

6 Which two sentences are out of order? _____

_____

7 If you were revising this paragraph, where would you place these two sentences?

_____

_____

6 Read this paragraph carefully.

The ideal house for me would be in the country where it's peaceful and pollution-free. It would be a two-story house with large white columns in front. There would be a fireplace between the den and living room. I would have a large master bedroom with sliding glass doors. I would like a study where I could transact all my business deals. I also want a ten-acre lake, and a basement for my pool table and my model train hobby.

1 This paragraph may seem unconnected because no transitions are used to help establish the location of the descriptive detail. Which of the following transitions could you use to signal spatial relationships to the reader?

On the first floor	Near the bedroom
On the second floor	Past the lake
At the front of the house	Underneath the first floor

Insert the appropriate transitions into the paragraph where you think they belong.

2 Write a good concluding sentence for this paragraph. _____

_____

110

3 Which detail does the writer really consider the most important? _____

_____

_____

7 Read the paragraph carefully.

The ideal car for me wouldn't really be a car; it would be a van. I'm saving my money now for a custom van with a metallic paint job and wide tires on mag wheels. I want a picture window and big spoilers. I want a painted mural. I need full carpeting and a small bed, a bar complete with a refrigerator, and a television and a full stereo system. There will be swiveling captain's chairs and a custom control console with a wooden-rimmed steering wheel. The engine will be turbocharged with adjustable boost and will have a racing cam, high compression pistons, transistorized ignition, and custom exhaust. I will have it balanced and detailed with braided metal fuel lines and electrical wiring.

1 Choose the appropriate transitions, and insert them in the paragraph.

On one side	on the other side
inside	front and rear
under the hood	in the driver's area
next to the passenger	near the bar

2 Describe the arrangement of the descriptive detail. _____

_____

3 Which details does the writer consider most important?

_____

_____

_____

_____

_____

4 Write a good concluding sentence for this paragraph. _____

_____

_____

_____

_____

Readings

Battle Scene

John Steinbeck

8 The following paragraphs are samples from the essay that begins on page 114. By reading these paragraphs and answering the questions, you will prepare yourself to read and understand the entire essay more easily.

He would have smelled the sharp <u>cordite</u> in the air and the hot <u>reek</u> of blood if the going has been rough. The burning odor of dust will be in his nose and the stench of men and animals killed yesterday and the day before. Then a whole building is blown up and an earthy, sour smell comes from its walls. He will smell his own sweat and the <u>accumulated</u> sweat of an army. When his throat is dry he will drink warm water from his canteen, which tastes of <u>disinfectant</u>.

While the correspondent is writing for you of advances and retreats, his skin will be raw from the woolen clothes he has not taken off for three days and his feet will be hot and dirty and swollen from not having taken off his shoes for days. He will itch from last night's mosquito bites and today's sand-fly bites. Perhaps he will have a little sand-fly fever, so that his head pulses and a red rim comes into his vision. His head may ache from the heat and his eyes burn with the dust. The knee that was sprained when he leaped ashore will grow stiff and painful, but it is no wound and cannot be treated.

Reading for Meaning

1 Locate the underlined words in the paragraph, and reread the sentences in which they appear. Write your own definition of what the word means in that sentence. Use a dictionary if necessary.

cordite _____

reek _____

accumulated _____

disinfectant _____

Reading for Structure

2 Does the first paragraph have a topic sentence? _____

3 List its details. These details describe the impact of a battle scene on which senses?

_____

_____

_____

4 Does the second paragraph have a topic sentence? _____

5 List the details in this paragraph. The impressions of which senses are being given here?

_____

_____

_____

_____

6 Are there any transitions between these supporting details? List them.

_____

_____

9 Now read the entire essay "Battle Scene" with the sample paragraphs in place.

[1] You can't see much of a battle. Those paintings <u>reproduced</u> in history books which show long lines of advancing troops, <u>close massed</u>, and being received by massed defending troops, are either <u>idealized</u> or else times and battles have changed. The account in the morning papers of the battle of yesterday was not seen by the correspondent, but was put together from reports.

114

[2] What the correspondent really saw was dust and the nasty burst of shells, low bushes and slit trenches. He lay on his stomach, if he had any sense, and watched ants crawling among the little sticks on the sand dune, and his nose was so close to the ants that their progress was interfered with by it.

[3] Then he saw an advance. Not straight lines of men marching into cannon fire, but little groups scuttling like crabs from bits of cover to other cover, while the high chatter of machine guns sounded, and the deep proom of shellfire.

[4] Perhaps the correspondent scuttled with them and hit the ground again. His report will be of battle plan and tactics, of taken ground or lost terrain, of attack and counterattack. But these are some of the things he probably really saw:

[5] He might have seen the splash of dirt and dust that is a shell burst, and a small Italian girl in the street with her stomach blown out, and he might have seen an American soldier standing over a twitching body, crying. He probably saw many dead mules, lying on their sides, reduced to pulp. He saw the wreckage of houses with torn beds hanging like shreds out of the spilled hole in a plaster wall. There were red carts and the stalled vehicles of refugees who did not get away.

[6] The stretcher-bearers come back from the lines, walking in off step, so that the burden will not be jounced too much, and the blood dripping from the canvas, brother and enemy in the stretchers, so long as they are hurt. And the walking wounded coming back with shattered arms and bandaged heads, the walking wounded struggling painfully to the rear.

[7] He would have smelled the sharp cordite in the air and the hot reek of blood if the going has been rough. The burning odor of dust will be in his nose and the stench of men and animals killed yesterday and the day before. Then a whole building is blown up and an earthy, sour smell comes from its walls. He will smell his own sweat and the accumulated sweat of an army. When his throat is dry he will drink warm water from his canteen, which tastes of disinfectant.

[8] While the correspondent is writing for you of advances and retreats, his skin will be raw from the woolen clothes he has not taken off for three days, and his feet will be hot and dirty and swollen from not having taken off his shoes for days. He will itch from last night's mosquito bites and from today's sand-fly bites. Perhaps he will have a little sand-fly fever, so that his head pulses and a red rim comes into his vision. His head may ache from the heat and his eyes burn with the dust. The knee that was sprained when he leaped ashore will grow stiff and painful, but it is no wound and cannot be treated.

115

[9] "The 5th Army advanced two kilometers," he will write, while the lines of trucks churn the road to deep dust and truck drivers hunch over their wheels. And off to the right the burial squads are scooping slits in the sandy earth. Their <u>charges</u> lie huddled on the ground and before they are laid in the sand, the second of the two dog tags is detached so that you know that that man with that army serial number is dead and out of it.

[10] These are the things he sees while he writes of tactics and strategy and names generals and in print decorates heroes. He takes a heavily waxed box from his pocket. That is his dinner. Inside there are two little packets of hard cake which have the flavor of dog biscuits. There is a tin can of cheese and a roll of vitamin-charged candy, an envelope of lemon powder to make the canteen water taste less bad and a tiny package of four cigarettes.

[11] That is dinner, and it will keep him moving for several more hours and keep his stomach working and his heart pumping. And if the line has advanced beyond him while he eats, dirty, buglike children will sidle up to him cringing and sniffling, their noses ringed with flies, and these children will whine for one of the hard biscuits and some of the vitamin candy. They will cry for candy: "Caramela—caramela—caramela—O.K., O.K., shank you, good-by." And if he gives the candy to one, the ground will <u>spew</u> up more dirty, buglike children, and they will scream shrilly, "Caramela—caramela." The correspondent will get the <u>communiqué</u> and will write your morning <u>dispatch</u> on his creaking, dust-filled portable, "General Clark's 5th Army advanced two kilometers against heavy artillery fire yesterday."

Reading for Meaning

1 Locate the underlined words in the essay, and reread the sentences in which they appear. Write your own definition of what the word means in that sentence. Use a dictionary if necessary.

reproduced _____

close massed _____

idealized _____

terrain _____

pulp _____

refugees _____

charges _____

spew _____

communiqué _____

dispatch _____

Reading for Structure

2 What is the topic developed in paragraph 3? _____

3 What details describe the advance? _____

4 What is the topic developed in paragraphs 5 and 6? _____

_____

5 Which sentence is the topic sentence for these two paragraphs?

_____

6 List the transitions that link the descriptive details in these paragraphs.

_____

7 What are the topics developed in paragraph 9? _____

8 What transition is needed to move the reader from one topic to the next in paragraph 9?

_____

9 What topic is developed in paragraph 10? _____

10 Which is the topic sentence? _____

11 What transition moves the reader from the battle scene to the description of the correspondent's dinner?

_____

_____

12 Which is the first sentence of descriptive detail? What aspect of the dinner does it describe?

_____

_____

13 What transition word introduces the rest of the descriptive detail? _____

14 List the transitions that link the descriptive detail in the rest of the paragraph.

_____

_____

15 What is the subject of paragraph 11? _____

16 What transition moves the reader from dinner to this topic?

_____

17 What function does the final sentence in the selection perform?

_____

_____

_____

Comprehension Test

18 In paragraph 1, how does Steinbeck say historical accounts of battles come about? Why?

_____

_____

_____

19 In paragraph 2, Steinbeck describes the correspondent lying on the ground watching ants on the dunes. What facts about ants make this scene important?

_____

_____

_____

20 According to paragraph 5, what are some effects of a shell burst?

_____

_____

21 Why is the American soldier crying in paragraph 5? _____

_____

22 Are the stretcher-bearers sympathetic to the wounded they carry? Why?

_____

_____

_____

23 In paragraph 7, Steinbeck attempts to describe the smell of a battlefield. What are some of the smells he describes?

119

24 What kinds of physical discomforts does the correspondent have to endure?

25 What effects does sand-fly fever have on a person? _____

26 Why is the "second of the two dog tags" detached from the bodies of soldiers before burial?

27 Describe a typical dinner for the correspondent.

28 Where do you think the children in paragraph 11 come from? Why are they alone?

29 Does Steinbeck think history provides a true account of war? What does history leave out?

30 What does Steinbeck think is most important in reporting a

battle? _____

_____

31 What is Steinbeck's attitude toward war? _____

_____

_____

Writing Assignments

32 Using paragraph 5 as a model, write your own paragraph describing a scene that frightens you.

_____

_____

_____

_____

_____

_____

_____

_____

_____

_____

_____

_____

_____

_____

_____

_____

_____

_____

_____

_____

_____

_____

_____

_____

_____

33 Write a paragraph describing another scene or situation that is often idealized or reported falsely.

_____

_____

_____

_____

_____

_____

_____

_____

_____

_____

_____

_____

_____

_____

_____

_____

_____

_____

_____

_____

_____

_____

_____

_____

_____

_____

34 Write a paragraph describing how someone _might_ describe this classroom if he wanted to idealize it.

_____

_____

_____

_____

_____

_____

_____

_____

_____

Readings _____

The Birth of the
United States

Jim Bishop

10   The following paragraphs are samples from the essay that begins on page 127. By reading these paragraphs and answering the questions, you will prepare yourself to read and understand the entire essay more easily.

     The city, stretching a mile and a half in one direction and a mile in the other, was as busy as a hive. That small space, smaller than the 7,500 acres his father had left him at Monticello, Virginia, had a population of 38,000—second only to the great metropolis of London.

     As he walked, his blue eyes captured the drays bringing produce to the city on Monday morning, the heavy wagons hauled by plodding oxen yanking hogsheads of beer and spirits; black slaves with hands on hips carrying baskets of laundry on their heads; the businessmen with broad-brimmed beaver hats hurrying to and from their offices; bearded sailors in rough homespun, gawking at the heat-shimmering skyline of Philadelphia.

Reading for Meaning

1   Locate the underlined words in the paragraphs, and reread the sentences in which they appear. Write your own definition of what the word means in that sentence. Use a dictionary if necessary.

metropolis _____

drays _____

hogshead _____

gawking _____

heat-shimmering _____

Reading for Structure

2 What topic is developed in these two paragraphs? _____

3 Which sentence is the topic sentence? _____

4 Why are there two paragraphs instead of a single one describing the city?

_____

_____

5 How are the topics of the two paragraphs different? _____

_____

6 If the paragraphs were combined into a single paragraph, what transition words or phrases could keep the two subdivisions of the topic separate?

_____   _____

_____   _____

7 List the details used to describe the streets of the city and to develop the topic sentence's assertion that the city was "busy as a hive."

_____

_____

_____

_____

8 Would the paragraph be a better one—that is, better developed and more formal—if the two parts of it were combined? Why?

_____

_____

126

1 Now read the entire essay "The Birth of the United States" with the sample paragraphs in place.

[1] The tall redhead emerged from his parlor and bedroom with a big brass key and a large squarish object which looked like an easel. He locked the door and slipped the key into his waistcoat pocket. Thomas Jefferson, an intellectual at age thirty-three, was disappointed with these rooms.

[2] He had selected the new, three-story brick house at Market and Seventh streets in Philadelphia because there were no other homes or businesses near it and he had counted on "a freely circulating air," which had not <u>asserted</u> itself in the deathly stillness of hot June nights and the swarms of mosquitoes which seemed addicted to human ears.

[3] He stepped out into the <u>brassy</u> morning sun which stood above the trees on the Delaware River. He walked down Seventh Street toward the State House; Jefferson did not complain to bricklayer Jacob Graff, the young man who had built the house.

[4] He was not a complainer, even when he had a legitimate complaint. His peers among the statesmen of the Colonies saw Thomas Jefferson as a shy man, an <u>introvert</u> who could write with a degree of majestic philosophy, but who would not defend what he had written.

[5] There was a chance, he knew, that if the Colonies voted independence of the British Crown, this city of Philadelphia might be the capital of a new nation, or of a <u>conglomerate</u> of states.

[6] The city, stretching a mile and a half in one direction and a mile in the other, was as busy as a hive. That small space, smaller than the 7,500 acres his father had left him at Monticello, Virginia, had a population of 38,000—second only to the great metropolis of London.

[7] As he walked, his blue eyes captured the drays bringing produce to the city on Monday morning, the heavy wagons hauled by plodding oxen yanking hogsheads of beer and spirits; black slaves with hands on hips carrying baskets of laundry on their heads; the businessmen with broad-brimmed beaver hats hurrying to and from their offices; bearded sailors in rough home-spun, gawking at the heat-shimmering skyline of Philadelphia.

[8] Stout housewives in long swirling skirts, lace handkerchiefs pinned to their hair, curled by Jefferson on the pedestrian path, some turning to look at the "easel." They could believe that the freckled redhead was an artist; certainly he

looked like any other stranger in the city except that his gray breeches and gray waistcoat with the robin's-egg blue facing were too proper a uniform for an artist.

[9] It was not given to any of them to know that the "easel" was an invention of Jefferson's. It was a portable desk with ratchets. When it was set upon the knees, the upper leaf could be raised to 35 degrees of upright.

[10] Nor would any but Jefferson know that, this morning, the "easel" contained an instrument which he had devised entitled "THE UNANIMOUS DECLARATION of the thirteen united STATES OF AMERICA." It would be read today by the clerk of the Second Continental Congress. Afterward, few of the delegates would resist the temptation to shred, to alter, to <u>obliterate</u> the high-blown philosophical phrases.

Reading for Meaning

1 Locate the underlined words in the essay, and reread the sentences in which they appear. Write your own definition of what the word means in that sentence. Use a dictionary if necessary.

asserted _____

brassy _____

introvert _____

conglomerate _____

obliterate _____

Reading for Structure

2 The excerpt may have led you to believe that this selection would be a description of a city. What is actually the subject of the complete essay?

_____

3 Which paragraph serves as a transition to the two paragraphs

describing Philadelphia?_____

128

4 Which sentence serves as a transition from the description of Philadelphia back to the subject of Jefferson and his easel?

_____

5 What is the topic described in paragraph 9? _____

6 Does this paragraph have a topic sentence? _____

7 List the details that are given to describe the easel. _____

_____

8 What is the subject of paragraph 10? _____

9 Does this paragraph have a topic sentence? _____

_____

10 What is the topic described in paragraph 4? _____

11 Which sentence in this paragraph is the topic sentence?

_____

12 List the details used to describe Jefferson in this paragraph.

_____

13 Which of these details is repeated in the last sentence of the selection?

_____

14 The paragraphs describe first Jefferson's rooms, then Jefferson himself, the city of Philadelphia, the easel, and the Declaration of Independence. Are the descriptions arranged according to any particular order? What is their order?

_____

_____

15 List all the transitions you find that relate these descriptive paragraphs to each other and that keep them separate for the reader.

_____

_____

_____

Comprehension Test

16 What details about Jefferson's person are provided in paragraph 1?

_____

_____

_____

17 Why did Jefferson choose his apartment? What disappointed him about it?

_____

_____

_____

18 Who built the house he is living in? _____

19 What city is being described in paragraph 3? _____

20 What river is near Philadelphia? _____

21 How large was Philadelphia in Jefferson's time? _____

_____

22 What was the population? _____

23 Describe a typical Monday morning in Philadelphia. _____

_____

_____

_____

_____

_____

24 What century is being discussed in the essay? How do you

know? _____

_____

_____

_____

_____

25 What about Jefferson's appearance made people stare? _____

_____

26 What was the "easel" Jefferson carried? _____

_____

27 What did the "easel" contain? _____

28 How does the author build up suspense about the "easel"? __

_____

_____

29 Were you aware of the purpose of the "easel" before the end of
the essay? Why?

_____

_____

_____

_____

_____

_____

Writing Assignments

30 Write a paragraph describing the main street of your hometown on a busy day.

_____

_____

_____

_____

_____

_____

_____

_____

_____

_____

_____

31 Write a paragraph describing an invention you would like to see created.

_____

_____

32 Write a paragraph describing a person you know. Be very specific about the person's appearance.

_____

_____

_____

_____

_____

_____

_____

_____

_____

_____

_____

_____

_____

_____

_____

_____

_____

_____

_____

_____

_____

_____

Readings _____

From *Power*
Michael Korda

2 The following paragraph is a sample from the essay that begins on page 137. By reading this paragraph and answering the questions, you will prepare yourself to read and understand the entire essay more easily.

When the door opens, the captain himself appears, a lean, tall, handsome man in his early fifties, wearing a checked suit, a blue <u>linen</u> shirt, black patent leather Gucci loafers and a thin Florentine gold wrist watch which he never looks at. Mahoney has the rugged, expressive, and <u>self-deprecating</u> good looks of the young John Huston or Jason Robards, Jr.—one can imagine him easily as Hickey in *The Iceman Cometh.* The first thing that strikes one about him are his eyes, large, intelligent, <u>shrewd</u>, and of a dazzling blue <u>intensity</u> that is instantly persuasive and disarming. Mahoney seems to know how to use his eyes—he looks straight at you, doesn't ever seem to blink, leans forward across the table to bring them closer to you, twists himself in his chair to keep them at the level of yours. He has the quality of a hypnotist or an actor—there's something unlikely about him as a businessman, except that the eyes can go awfully cold when he's asking you questions. Mahoney is in constant motion, chain-smoking, pouring himself Sanka from a stainless steel coffeepot, gesturing, tilting his chair back, but his feet stay firmly planted on the floor, and he has the habit of pushing his belongings across the table very gradually, a gold lighter, his ashtray and his silver-plated mug making their way <u>inexorably</u> toward you as he talks.

Reading for Meaning

1 Locate the underlined words in the paragraph, and reread the sentences in which they appear. Write your own definition of what the word means in the sentence. Use a dictionary if necessary.

linen _____

self-deprecating _____

shrewd _____

intensity _____

inexorably _____

Reading for Structure

2 What is the topic developed in this sample paragraph? _____

3 What topic is developed in the first two sentences? _____

_____

4 What transition leads to the second subdivision, the subject of "his eyes"?

_____

5 What are the other general subdivisions of the topics developed in this paragraph?

_____

6 Are transitions placed between these other subdivisions? ___

7 Is there a topic sentence in this paragraph? _____

8 Write a topic sentence that will "sum up" the details given

here. _____

_____

_____

9 What is the main difference in development between this paragraph and the paragraphs in the preceding essay? What do you think accounts for the difference?

_____

_____

136

13 Now read the entire essay "From *Power*" with the sample paragraph in place.

[1] David Mahoney, the fifty-two-year-old chairman, president and chief executive officer of Norton Simon Inc. is "accustomed to the fast track." The track has always carried him toward power and success, and indeed he moved so fast and looked like such a winner that "the way has always been cleared for him by older men." The son of a Bronx construction worker thrown out of work by the Depression, Mahoney runs a conglomerate whose sales exceeded one and a half billion dollars in the fiscal year ending June 30, 1973, and whose activities include soft drinks, packaged foods, cosmetics, liquor, fashions, and magazines.

[2] The executive offices of Norton Simon Inc. on Park Avenue seem to have been designed to reflect the presence of power and money, in a quiet, self-assured style that is peculiarly late twentieth-century American. The "reception area" (it is far too big to be called a waiting room) is dimly lit, decorated in shades of brown, as silent and overpowering as a Pharaoh's tomb, and probably not much less expensive to build. The walls are hung with enormous abstract paintings, the kind of bland but costly art that is at once inoffensive and soothing, the carpet is a dark brown and beige basket-weave design, the furniture is stainless steel and leather—not so very different in spirit from a first-class passenger lounge at any airport—one almost expects to see a miniskirted waitress appear to take one's order and to hear the subdued moan of Muzak. What makes the difference is money. Everything here is solid and expensive, and despite the size of the rooms, one doubts that these chairs and couches are often occupied—they are here to fill up space.

[3] The corridors are equally dark and hermetic, though an open door reveals a glimpse of a surprisingly cheerful ladies' room, brilliantly lit and decorated in brightly modern flowered chintz and white plastic. Mahoney's own outer office is a big, quiet room with a spectacular view of New York, a conference table covered in painted blue linen, womb-like armchairs in tan suede leather, ornate cigarette boxes filled with Tareytons (Mahoney's brand), a table in fake alligator hide on which sits a copy of David Mahoney's interim report to the shareholders for the three months ending September 30, 1973, tastefully bound in blue-gray parchment paper. The white curtains sway gracefully in the breeze from the ventilating system, the windows are sealed, and from the other side of the door that leads to Mahoney's private office come the sounds of a spirited argu-

ment in which the phrase "operating capital" recurs frequently. It is like being in the control room of a spaceship starbound for profit.

[4] When the door opens, the captain himself appears, a lean, tall, handsome man in his early fifties, wearing a checked suit, a blue linen shirt, black patent leather Gucci loafers and a thin Florentine gold wrist watch which he never looks at. Mahoney has the rugged, expressive, and self-deprecating good looks of the young John Huston or Jason Robards, Jr.—one can imagine him easily as Hickey in *The Iceman Cometh.* The first thing that strikes one about him are his eyes, large, intelligent, shrewd, and of a dazzling blue intensity that is instantly persuasive and disarming. Mahoney seems to know how to use his eyes—he looks straight at you, doesn't ever seem to blink, leans forward across the table to bring them closer to you, twists himself in his chair to keep them at the level of yours. He has the quality of a hypnotist or an actor—there's something unlikely about him as a businessman, except that the eyes can go awfully cold when he's asking you questions. Mahoney is in constant motion, chain-smoking, pouring himself Sanka from a stainless steel coffeepot, gesturing, tilting his chair back, but his feet stay firmly planted on the floor, and he has the habit of pushing his belongings across the table very gradually, a gold lighter, his ashtray and his silver plated mug making their way inexorably toward you as he talks.

[5] It is difficult to imagine Mahoney radiating anything but vitality. His physical presence is striking—he is lean, tanned in mid-winter, one of those people who would attract attention anywhere. He has a charm like that of John F. Kennedy (another Irish American success story), although the only photographs in the room are two autographed color spreads of President and Mrs. Nixon from a *McCall's* story.

[6] "Power is a lever . . ." Mahoney says. We are chatting about his responsibilities, his <u>meteoric</u> career, and Mahoney is trying to define just how he got where he is. "Is power persuasion or force?" he asks, shrugging, "or <u>manipulation?</u>" He pauses to ask if I have read Alan Watts, gracefully works Newton's Third Law into his conversation, quoting it exactly, dismisses people who have disagreed with him with a genial "God bless' em," picks up a phone and says, "Tell them it's for six o'clock and we're going to have to move them back," then he goes on to discuss how he runs his business. For Mahoney sees power as a means of getting things done, is uncomfortable with the idea of power as an abstraction, a quality he has rather than a working tool. He is interested, as he says, in "how, not why."

[7] "There's no <u>autonomy</u> in the world," he says. "There are damn few things I could just do. Do I feel that I want to run things, and make the decisions? Yes. But I've always been a line operator." He pauses. "Basically, for all the companies I've worked for, I've had to be a moneymaker. There has to be a leader to make things work, somebody who has whatever that <u>intangible</u> quality is." Mahoney searches for an example, obviously reluctant to use himself. "Joe Namath!" he says. "He had the power; he was a leader." Mahoney smiles broadly, and I understand why Namath comes to his mind, for Mahoney excelled at baseball and basketball at Cathedral High School in Manhattan, and realized that skill and the will to win in athletics was the only way he would ever get a college education. Playing basketball to win took him to the University of Pennsylvania's Wharton School and, in a sense, finally to this office. He is still playing to win, and has a fellow feeling for athletic stars, whose problems on the field he likes to compare to his own. So far as his own success is concerned, he is content to say that "Ever since Moses came down from the mountain with the tablets, the world has been moved by salesmen. I'm a salesman."

[8] As to running a company, Mahoney sees his role as getting the best out of people, a form of salesmanship itself. He likes "to <u>ratify</u> good decisions, not make them, to <u>orchestrate</u> people," but one can imagine that he has no trouble in orchestrating them toward the decision he wants made, and he does not deny a capacity to manipulate people and enforce discipline. "I much prefer a <u>consensus</u>," he says, "but I don't trust total agreement. If two people agree all the time, one of them is unnecessary."

[9] On the question of using his power toughly, Mahoney is ever so slightly <u>evasive</u>, in part because of the story of a power game he is said to have played on the executive who had been running Norton Simon Inc.'s Canada Dry division for two weeks. When the latter pointed out that the division couldn't possibly meet its figures for the year, Mahoney told him to "be on budget by the six-month mark." When he asked what would happen if he couldn't make it, Mahoney is said to have replied, "Then clean out your desk and go home."

[10] This story worries Mahoney a lot, and he is at pains to point out that the Canada Dry executive did in fact "make his figures," and is still with the company. "These things aren't personal. What I want to know is not why you are down, it's When are you going to be up? Give me the how, not the why. I'm prepared to listen to the reasons, and I can understand good

reasons, like a strike in a bottling plant, but I want to know how you're going to climb out of something like that. If you can't make it you'd better have a damn good reason and a plan." For the first time, a hint of Mahoney's toughness shows through as he dismisses the subject abruptly: "Anyway, he agreed to those figures, they were his figures!"

[11] Figures play a large part in Mahoney's conversation, and in fact he explains his own position by saying, "All I am is the sum total of everybody else's figures." How does he <u>ensure</u> that everybody meets their figures? Mahoney talks about "the process of getting things done," about persuasion, <u>incentives</u> ("You fill people's needs for money, security, whatever it is, everybody wants something, after all, even if it's only a good table at the Pump Room"), then reluctantly considers the possibility that his power relies on an element of fear. "People fear things, sure, they sometimes fear me. You fear anyone or anything that can cause you a problem. People's fear of me is really their fear of themselves. If they're performing, they don't have anything to fear. There's probably fear in every organization, and it's natural. The first time you disagree with the boss the fear starts. It can't be helped."

[12] Mahoney quickly points out that the constructive use of power is not easy for him. He dislikes firing people—"It's the most difficult decision, hard enough when it's people you know and like—you know their wives, homes, children—but it's even harder when it's people you don't know, when you close down a whole plant because you have to." For a moment he looks grim, perhaps it's a decision he's in the process of making, then he smiles suddenly and adds, "You have to take the job seriously, but not take yourself seriously. Otherwise work is a drudge."

[13] How does Mahoney feel about money? Did he always want power, wealth, success? "I just always knew I never wanted to be poor," he says, and recalls seeing a limousine waiting outside a theater when he was a child and thinking it meant "power and security." He rises to his feet without having looked at his watch, apparently aware that it is nearly six o'clock. "But limousines and things like that wear off," he adds. "You get a lot of <u>perquisites</u>, and they're important to your <u>ego</u>. To me, it goes back to the money end of it. I don't want it to be unrewarded. I've earned it." He apologizes for leaving, but has an exercise class at Alex and Walter's Gym at six-thirty, and the limousine is waiting downstairs. At the door he pauses and turns back. "With power comes responsibility," he says in-

tently. "When you have a string on the company—it has a string on you." And he's gone, moving with the graceful speed of an old athlete.

Reading for Meaning

1 Locate the underlined words in the essay, and reread the sentences in which they appear. Write your own definition of what the word means in that sentence. Use a dictionary if necessary.

conglomerate _____

fiscal _____

bland _____

subdued _____

hermetic _____

chintz _____

ornate _____

interim _____

spirited _____

meteoric _____

manipulation _____

autonomy _____

intangible _____

ratify _____

orchestrate _____

consensus _____

The words in the left-hand column are underlined in the essay. Reread the sentences in which they appear, and pick, from the choices at the right, the word that is closest in meaning. Circle your answer.

evasive	dishonest	dodging the point	outspoken
ensure	protect	cover	guarantee
incentives	rewards	stimuli	aromas
perquisites	profits	necessities	prejudices
ego	status	occupation	self-esteem

Reading for Structure

2 What topic is described in paragraph 2? _____

3 Which is the topic sentence of paragraph 2? _____

4 List the details used to describe the reception area in the order they are given.

_____

_____

5 What topic is described in paragraph 3? _____

6 Which is the topic sentence in paragraph 3? _____

7 What transition sentence moves the reader from the "reception area" to Mahoney's offices?

_____

8 List the details used to describe Mahoney's office in the order they are given.

_____

_____

142

9 Paragraph 5 begins by describing Mahoney's "vitality." How does this paragraph also function as a transition to paragraph 6, which describes Mahoney and "power"?

_____

_____

10 The rest of this selection actually is a report of an interview with Mahoney, describing him by describing his ideas about himself and his power. How are these paragraphs and their details arranged?

_____

_____

11 Find and list the transitions that signal this arrangement to the reader.

_____

_____

Comprehension Test

12 Who is David Mahoney? _____

13 Describe the office of Norton Simon Inc. _____

_____

_____

_____

14 Describe Mahoney's office. _____

_____

_____

_____

_____

_____

15 Describe Mahoney's appearance. _____

_____

16 How does Mahoney conduct himself in conferences? _____

_____

_____

17 How does Mahoney run his business? _____

_____

_____

18 What is the function of "fear" in supervising people? _____

_____

_____

19 What information in the essay shows that Mahoney is sympathetic toward people?

_____

_____

20 How does Mahoney feel about money? _____

_____

21 What is the main idea of this essay? Explain. _____

_____

_____

_____

_____

_____

_____

Writing Assignments

22   Write a paragraph describing a person you consider powerful.

_____

_____

_____

_____

_____

_____

_____

_____

_____

_____

_____

_____

_____

_____

_____

_____

_____

_____

_____

_____

_____

_____

_____

_____

_____

_____

_____

_____

23 Write a paragraph describing the job you would like to have after college.

_____

_____

_____

_____

_____

_____

_____

_____

_____

_____

_____

_____

_____

_____

_____

_____

_____

_____

Readings_____

The Spring,
The Garden,
The Outbuildings

James Agee

14 The following paragraph is a sample from the essay that begins on page 150. By reading this paragraph and answering the questions, you will prepare yourself to read and understand the entire essay more easily.

The smokehouse is about eight feet square and about seven tall to the peak of the roof. It is built of <u>vertical</u> boards of <u>uniform</u> width. The door is <u>flush</u> to the wall without a frame and is held shut by a wood button. On the uphill side, at center of the wall and flat to it, hangs a nearly new washtub, the <u>concentrics</u> on its bottom circle like a target. Its <u>galvanized</u> material is brilliant and dryly heating in the sun; the wood of the wall itself is not much less brilliant. The natural usage of a smokehouse is to smoke and store meat, but meat is not smoked here: this is a storage house. Mainly, there are a couple of dozen tin cans here, of many differing sizes and former uses, now holding sorghum; four hoes; a set of sweeps; a broken plow-frame; pieces of an ice-cream freezer; a can of rusty nails; a number of mule shoes; the strap of a white slipper; a pair of greenly eaten, crumpled work-shoes, the uppers broken away, the soles worn broadly through, still carrying the odor of feet; a blue coil of soft iron wire; a few yards of rusted barbed wire; a rotted mule-collar; pieces of wire at random: all those same broken creatures of the Ricketts' porch of uselessness and of almost endless saving.

Reading for Meaning

1 Locate the underlined words in the paragraph, and reread the sentences in which they appear. Write your own definition of what the word means in that sentence. Use a dictionary if necessary.

vertical _____

uniform _____

flush _____

concentrics_____

galvanized _____

Reading for Structure

2 What is the topic developed in this paragraph? _____

3 In which sentences is the reader given details about the exterior of the smokehouse?

_____

4 List the details given that describe the exterior appearance of the smokehouse.

_____

_____

5 In which sentences is the reader given details about the interior of the smokehouse?

_____

6 List the details that describe the interior of the smokehouse.

_____

_____

7 Which sentence separates the two sections of the paragraph that deal with the exterior and interior details?

_____

8 Is there a topic sentence for this paragraph?_____

9 This is one of the longest, most fully developed paragraphs you have read; most of the other paragraphs in the selection from which it is taken are also long. Why do you think this paragraph and the others you will read are so fully developed? How is their development related to the author's purpose?

---

15   Now read the entire essay "The Spring, The Garden, The Outbuildings" with the sample paragraph in place.

[1] The spring is out to the rear of the house and above it, about a hundred and fifty yards away to the right, not a short distance to walk for every drop of water that is needed. The path lifts from the end of the back hall between the henroost and the smokehouse to just below the barn, swings left here, parts from the hill path, and runs narrowly, but slick as a scalp, among thick weeds under sunlight and toward trees whose green-brown gloom and coolness is sudden and whose silence, different from that of the open light, seems to be <u>conscious</u> and to await the <u>repetition</u> of a signal. Not five feet deeper, a delicate yet powerful <u>odor</u> of wetness in constant shade, a broad windless standing-forth of a new coolness as from a refrigerator door, and a <u>diminutive</u> wrinkling noise of water: and ten feet deep within the roof of leaves, low, on the upward right, the spring, the dirt all round dark and <u>strong-rooted</u> and fragrant, tamped smooth as soap with bare feet, and a <u>mottled</u> piece of plank to kneel to water on. The water stands forward from between rounded <u>strata</u> of submerged dark stone as from between lips of rollers, in a look not of motion yet of quiet <u>compulsion</u>, into a basin a foot deep floored with dead oakleaves and shored up with slimy wood. On a submerged shelf small crocks of butter, cream, and milk stand sunken to their eyes, tied over with pieces of <u>saturated</u> floursack. A sapling next the spring has been chopped short to make a stob, and on it hangs a coffee can rusted black and split at the edges. The spring is now <u>cowled</u> so deeply under the hill that the water is brilliant and nervy, seeming to break in the mouth like crystals, as spring water can: it is about the temper of faucet water, and tastes slack and faintly sad, and as if just short of stale. It is not quite <u>tepid</u>, however, and it does not seem to taste of sweat and sickness, as the water does which the Woods family have to use.

[2] Ten feet below, in a little <u>alcove</u> cleared at the edge of the woods, the water lets out through a rusted pipe and rambles

loose. There is a brute oak bench here for washtubs, and burnt stones are squared round the bright ashes of wood fires, and next to these stones is one of those very heavy and handsome black iron kettles in which people one remove more primitive still make their own soap.

[3] So, at the end of a slim <u>liana</u> of dry path running out of the heart of the house, a small wet flower suspended: the spring.

[4] The garden plot is close on the right rear of the house. It is about the shape and about two thirds the size of a tennis court, and is caught within <u>palings</u> against the hunger and damage of animals. These palings are thin slats of split pine about three and a half feet tall and an inch and a half wide, wired together vertically, about their width apart from each other. The <u>erratic</u> grain and <u>cleavage</u> of this pine have given each of them a different <u>welter</u> and rippling streaming of surface and pattern structure; the weather has made this all as it were a muted silver and silk, exquisitely sensitive to light; and these slats closely approximate yet seldom perfect their perpendiculars; so that when the sun is on them, and with the segments of garden between each of them, there is here such a <u>virtuosity</u> as might be watched by speechless days on end merely for the variety and distinction of their beauty, without thought or any relevant room for thinking, and without possibility of absorbing all that is there to be seen. Outside, the <u>frowsy</u> weeds stand halfway up these walls: inside, the planting is concentrated to the utmost possible, in green and pink-veined wax and velvet butter beans, and in rank tomatoes, hung low, burst against the ground, in hairy buds of okra, all these sprung heavy with weeds and smothered in textured shades of their leaves, blown like nearly exploding balloons in the full spread of the summer, each in its shape and nature, so that the whole of this space is one <u>blowsy</u> bristling pool and splendor of worm-and-insect-embroidered plants and the savage odors of their special lusts that sting the face in gathering, nuzzling the paling as the bars of a zoo: waist-deep to wade in, so twined and spired and reached among each other that the paths between rows are discernible only like steps <u>confounded</u> in snow: a paling gate, nearest the kitchen, is bound shut against their bursting with a piece of wire.

[5] Behind the house the dirt is blond and bare, except a little fledging of grass-leaves at the roots of structures, and walked-out rags of grass thickening along the sides. It lifts up gently, perhaps five feet in twenty yards: across the top line of this twenty yards is the barn, set a few feet to the right of center of

the rear of the house. Half between the barn and house, sym-
metrical to the axis of the house, the henroost and the smokehouse face each other across a bare space of perhaps twelve
feet of dirt.

[6] These, like the house, are all made of unpainted pine. In
some of this wood, the grain is broad and distinct: in some of
it the grain has almost disappeared, and the wood has a texture
and look like that of weathered bone.

[7] The henroost is about seven feet square and five high,
roofed with rotted shingles. It is built rather at random of
planks varying in width between a foot and four inches, nailed
on horizontally with narrow spaces between their edges. On the
uphill side a short pole leans against the roof with chips and
sticks nailed along it for steps and a box nailed at the top with
straw in it; but most of the eggs are found by the children in
places which are of the hens' own selection and return. Inside
the roost, three or four sections of saplings, so arranged that the
hens will not dirty each other; these poles rubbed smooth by
their feet; the strong slits of light between the boards; the odor
of closured and heated wood; and the nearly unbearably fetid
odor of the feathers and excretions of the hens.

[8] The smokehouse is about eight feet square and about
seven tall to the peak of the roof. It is built of vertical boards
of uniform width. The door is flush to the wall without a frame
and is held shut by a wood button. On the uphill side, at center
of the wall and flat to it, hangs a nearly new washtub, the
concentrics on its bottom circle like a target. Its galvanized
material is brilliant and dryly heating in the sun; the wood of
the wall itself is not much less brilliant. The natural usage of
a smokehouse is to smoke and store meat, but meat is not
smoked here: this is a storage house. Mainly, there are a couple
of dozen tin cans here, of many differing sizes and former uses,
now holding sorghum; four hoes; a set of sweeps; a broken
plow-frame; pieces of an ice-cream freezer; a can of rusty nails;
a number of mule shoes; the strap of a white slipper; a pair of
greenly eaten, crumpled work-shoes, the uppers broken away,
the soles worn broadly through, still carrying the odor of feet;
a blue coil of soft iron wire; a few yards of rusted barbed wire;
a rotted mule-collar; pieces of wire at random: all those same
broken creatures of the Ricketts' porch of uselessness and of
almost endless saving.

[9] It should hardly be called a "barn," it is too thin an ex-
cuse for one: a long low shed divided into three chambers, a
wired in yard, a hog wallow and the hog's dirty little house. One

room is made of thick and thin logs, partly stopped with clay, and this is the stall for the mule when he is there: the rest is pine boards. The next partition is for the cow. In one corner of the small wired yard which squares off this part of the barn, in somewhat trampled and dunged earth, is the hogpen, made of logs; beyond that, a room used, in turn as a corncrib and as a storage house for cotton prior to ginning. There is no hayloft. The whole structure is about twenty feet long and not more than seven high and seven or eight deep. The floor, except for the corncrib, is earth.

[10] Here I must say a little anyhow: what I can hardly hope to bear out in the record: that a house of simple people which stands empty and silent in the vast Southern country morning sunlight, and everything which on this morning in eternal space it by chance contains, all thus left open and defenseless to a <u>reverent</u> and cold-laboring spy, shines quietly forth such <u>grandeur</u>, such sorrowful holiness of its <u>exactitudes</u> in existence, as no human consciousness shall ever rightly perceive, far less impart to another: that there can be more beauty and more deep wonder in the standings and spacings of mute furnishings on a bare floor between the squaring <u>bourns</u> of walls than in any music ever made: that this square home, as it stands in unshadowed earth between the winding years of heaven, is, not to me but of itself, one among the serene and final, uncapturable beauties of existence: that this beauty is made between hurt but <u>invincible</u> nature and the plainest cruelties and needs of human existence in this uncured time, and is <u>inextricable</u> among these, and as impossible without them as a saint born in paradise.

[11] But I say these things only because I am <u>reluctant</u> to entirely lie. I can have nothing more to do with them now. I am hoping here only to tell a little, only so well as I may, about an ordinary house, in which I lived a little while, and which is the home, for the time being, of the Gudger family, and is the sort of home a tenant family lives in, furnished and decorated as they furnish and decorate. Since it is so entirely <u>static</u> a subject, it may be slow going. That is as it may be.

Reading for Meaning

1 Locate the underlined words in the essay, and reread the sentences in which they appear. Write your own definition of what the word means in that sentence. Use a dictionary if necessary.

conscious _____

repetition _____

diminutive _____

strong-rooted _____

mottled _____

strata _____

compulsion _____

saturated _____

cowled _____

tepid _____

alcove _____

liana _____

palings _____

erratic _____

cleavage _____

The words in the left-hand column are underlined in the essay.
Reread the sentences in which they appear, and pick, from the
choices at the right, the word that is closest in meaning. Circle
your answer.

welter	disorder	wallow	wetness
virtuosity	merit	morality	great skill
frowsy	uncared for	windblown	puffy
blowsy	windy	disheveled	coarse
confounded	shamed	confused	damned
symmetrical	of equal distance	circling	adjacent to

fetid	offensive	moist	warm
reverent	resounding	daydreaming	respecting
grandeur	largeness	magnificence	soft light
exactitudes	examined	exactness	appropri-ateness
bourns	completion	streams	boundaries
invincible	sacred	unable to be seen	undefeat-able
inextricable	permanently entangled	indescribable	unerring
reluctant	hesitant	unwilling	opposed to
static	interference	weighty	stationary

Reading for Structure

2 What is the topic described in paragraph 1? _____

3 Why is the path described in the first section of paragraph 1?

_____

_____

4 List the details that are used to describe the spring. _____

_____

5 What transition introduces the topic of paragraph 2? _____

_____

6 What is the function of paragraph 3? _____

7 List all the transition words that indicate location in these first three paragraphs.

_____

_____

8 What topic is described in paragraph 4? _____

9 What part of this topic is described in the first four sentences in this paragraph?

_____

10 What part of this topic is described in the rest of the paragraph?

_____

_____

11 List the two transition words used in paragraph 4 to separate its two parts.

_____

12 What is the subject of paragraphs 5 to 10? Which paragraph lists them?

_____

_____

_____

13 What is the topic described in paragraph 7? _____

14 What part of the subject is described in the first three sentences? _____

15 What part of the subject is described in the rest of the paragraph? _____

_____

16 What transition word helps the reader with this division of the topic? _____

17 What is the topic described in paragraph 9? _____

18 Which sentence is the topic sentence?_____

19 Which sentence lists the subdivisions of the topic?_____

20 List the transitions that move the reader's attention from one part of the barn to the next.

_____

21 Is there a summary sentence? If so, which sentence is it?

_____

22 Why does the author wait to describe the exterior dimensions in almost the last sentence?

_____

23 This selection is from a longer essay. Judging by the last few paragraphs, what do you think the author intends to describe next?

_____

24 Paragraphs 9 to 11, then, conclude this short selection. What function do you think they serve in the complete essay?

_____

_____

Comprehension Test

25 Where is the spring located?_____

_____

26 What is the spring used for?_____

27 In your own words, describe the spring._____

_____

28 According to the passage, how does the water taste?_____

_____

29 Where is the garden located?_____

30 How large is the garden?_____

_____

31 In your own words, describe the fence that surrounds the garden._____

_____

_____

32 What kinds of vegetables are grown in the garden?_____

_____

33 Where are the henroost·and smokehouse located?_____

_____

34 In your own words, describe the henroost and smokehouse.

_____

_____

_____

_____

35 Name five things that are stored in the smokehouse._____

_____ _____ _____ _____

36 What structure that is not named in the title of this essay is

described in paragraph 9? _____

37 What meaning do you get from paragraph 10?_____

_____

_____

38 In paragraph 11, what reason does the author give for his vivid
descriptions of the farm?

_____

_____

39 How do you think the author feels about the farm he describes?
Why?

_____

_____

_____

40 The author describes five things in this passage (spring, barn,
henroost, garden, smokehouse). Put them in their order of description.

_____ _____ _____ _____

_____

41 The author's purpose in this essay is to portray as vividly as
possible the farm about which he is writing. Under each of the
following words, list five descriptive words that help you visu-
alize the subject:

spring   garden   henroost   smokehouse barn

_____   _____   _____   _____   _____

_____   _____   _____   _____   _____

_____   _____   _____   _____   _____

———   ———   ———   ———   ———

———   ———   ———   ———   ———

Writing Assignments

42 Write a paragraph describing the place where you study.

_____

_____

_____

_____

_____

_____

_____

_____

_____

_____

_____

_____

43 Write a paragraph describing where you live now for someone who's never been there.

_____

_____

_____

_____

_____

_____

_____

_____

_____

_____

_____

_____

_____

_____

_____

_____

_____

_____

_____

_____

_____

_____

_____

_____

_____

_____

44 Write a paragraph describing the desk at which you are sitting;
include the details of its appearance that make it different from
all the others in the room.

_____

_____

_____

_____

45 Write a paragraph describing the kitchen of your home for someone who has never been in your kitchen.

_____

_____

_____

_____

_____

_____

_____

_____

_____

_____

_____

_____

_____

_____

_____

_____

_____

_____

_____

_____

_____

4 Comparison - Contrast Arrangement of Detail

Another very common type of arrangement is comparison or contrast. A comparison paragraph or a contrast paragraph develops a topic by showing how it is like or unlike something else; so, in a sense, this sort of paragraph will actually have two topics rather than one. A comparison paragraph compares two topics that at first seem unlike each other, pointing out how they are actually similar. A contrast paragraph contrasts two topics that at first seem similar, pointing out how the two topics are actually unlike. Sometimes, though this is actually rare, a paragraph will point out both the similarities and differences of its two topics.

When a topic sentence is used in a comparison or contrast paragraph, it performs the same function it performs in other paragraphs. A topic sentence for a comparison or contrast paragraph will "announce" the two topics the paragraph will develop or describe, and it will make an assertion about them. The assertion will generally be that the two topics are alike (for a comparison paragraph) or unlike (for a contrast paragraph).

For example, consider this topic sentence from a paragraph on pet care:

Parakeets and canaries, though similar in appearance, are actually separate species and require different types of food and different treatment.

In this topic sentence, the two topics to be developed (parakeet care and canary care) are announced, and the reader is told that they are unlike. The paragraph to follow this sentence will be a contrast paragraph. On the other hand, consider this typical topic sentence:

Gerbils and white mice are very similar; the rules for raising either species are much the same.

In this sentence, again the two topics are announced, but in this case, the assertion is made that the two topics are similar. Therefore, the paragraph to follow this second topic sentence will be a comparison paragraph.

Comparison and contrast paragraphs are extremely useful to students, for many instructors give essay examinations that call for comparison or contrast of two topics. Examples of these sorts of assignments are: "Contrast the Mexican and American revolutions" or "Explain the difference between a neurosis and a psychosis." In addition, comparison and contrast reflect thinking processes we all engage in every day. Everytime you consider alternatives and choose between them—which car to buy, which perfume to wear, which course to take, whether to commute by car or bicycle—you compare or contrast the two topics.

Both comparison paragraphs and contrast paragraphs use many of the transitions used in other types of paragraphs. In addition, they may use some specialized transition words and phrases. Some of the transitions used to signal comparison are *likewise, also, too, similarly, like,* and *similar.* Some of the transitions used to signal contrast are *but, yet, in contrast, nevertheless, however, on the other hand,* and *on the contrary.*

When writing a comparison or contrast paragraph, you will often find it helpful to make a chart of the supporting detail you wish to include. For example, suppose you are asked to compare sports cars and exotic, 10-speed bicycles. You may know that both exotic cars and exotic bikes use lightweight metal alloys such as aluminum and magnesium, that both depend on special gearing for speed and power, and that the engineering in both are derived from racing models. A chart of your supporting detail might look like the one on page 166.

There are two ways in which this supporting detail can be arranged. The first method, continuous organization, treats each basis for comparison in turn and continuously moves from topic A to topic B. An outline for a paragraph on exotic cars and exotic bicycles using continuous organization would look like this:

1. Use of alloys
   A. in sports cars
   B. in bicycles

2. Use of special gearing
   A. in sports cars
   B. in bicycles

3. Derivation from racing
   models
   A. in sports cars
   B. in bicycles

As the paragraph is written, specific detail from the chart would be placed under each heading.

The second method, discontinuous organization, reverses this organization. In discontinuous organization, first topic A is described, then topic B. An outline for a paragraph on exotic bicycles that uses discontinuous organization would look like this:

A. Sports cars
   1. use of alloys
   2. use of special
      gearing
   3. derivation from
      racing models

B. Exotic bicycles
   1. use of alloys
   2. use of special
      gearing
   3. derivation from
      racing models

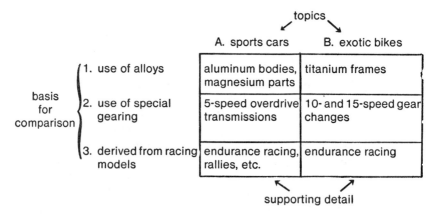

		topics	
		A. sports cars	B. exotic bikes
basis for comparison	1. use of alloys	aluminum bodies, magnesium parts	titanium frames
	2. use of special gearing	5-speed overdrive transmissions	10- and 15-speed gear changes
	3. derived from racing models	endurance racing, rallies, etc.	endurance racing

supporting detail

Section 3 COMPARISON-CONTRAST ARRANGEMENT OF DETAIL

Whichever arrangement is used, the reader must be helped to find his way by the use of transition words and phrases.

1 Now fill out this chart as if you were planning a paragraph to contrast two jobs you have had (or two jobs you might eventually have).

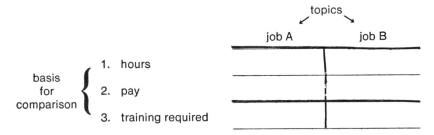

2 Fill out the outlines for continuous and discontinuous arrangement:

Discontinuous Organization

1. ———————————

    A. ———————————

    B. ———————————

2. ———————————

    A. ———————————

    B. ———————————

3. ———————————

    A. ———————————

    B. ———————————

Continuous Organization

A. ———————————

    1. ———————————

    2. ———————————

    3. ———————————

B. ———————————

    1. ———————————

    2. ———————————

    3. ———————————

3 Now, choose either continuous or discontinuous organization, and write out your paragraph. Be sure to use transitions to show contrast.

167

4 Read the following paragraph. Underline the topics being discussed.

According to Yiddish folk-wisdom, there are two types of jerks in the world, schlemiels and schlimazels, and the differences between them are easily understood. The schlemiel causes his own misadventures, either willfully or through his own inept behavior; the schlimazel is always an innocent victim—but somehow he always deserves his fate. A parable demonstrates the difference: the schlemiel orders a hot dog at a ball park, stands up to fumble for change (while blocking the view of those behind him), steps on peoples' feet as he struggles to reach for the hot dog, and then gapes in astonishment when at his first bite, the mustard-covered wiener squirts out of the hot dog bun. The schlimazel is the little guy in the white shirt that the wiener lands on.

1 Which sentence is the topic sentence? _____

2 What two topics are "announced" in the topic sentence? ____

_____

3 According to the topic sentence, are they to be compared or contrasted?

_____

_____

4 How is the supporting detail arranged? Is this continuous or

discontinuous organization? _____

_____

5 Write a concluding sentence for this paragraph. _____

_____

6 List the transition words and phrases used in this paragraph.

_____

_____

_____

5   Read the following paragraph, paying close attention to the organization of details.

Two places where I enjoy eating are the Orange Julius shop and the school cafeteria. The Orange Julius serves hot dogs, hamburgers, and other types of sandwiches, but you can't really get a balanced meal there. At the school cafeteria you can get meats, vegetables, salads, and dessert. At the Orange Julius shop the service is pretty fast, but you still have to wait while your order is prepared; at the school cafeteria you choose your meal from a buffet, walking down a line and choosing the dishes you want. You never have to wait for your food, because it's already cooked. The most important difference is the price of a meal. The prices for hot sandwiches are very high. The bill just for a hot dog, French fries, and soda comes to almost three dollars, whereas at the school cafeteria you can get a whole meal with dessert for only about two dollars.

1   Which sentence is the topic sentence? _____

2   Can you rewrite the topic sentence so that it indicates whether the two topics are to be compared or contrasted? _____

_____

_____

3   Is the supporting detail organized continuously or discontinuously? _____

4   List the transitions used in the paragraph._____

5   Where should these transitions be placed?

One difference is in the menus_____

On the other hand_____

At the Orange Julius_____

Another difference is the serving time._____

170

6 Write a good concluding sentence for this paragraph.

_____

_____

5 Read the following paragraph. Underline the two topics being discussed.

College life has been a far cry from my whole high school education. The main differences are in teachers, courses, and the time demands. The teachers in college are better trained than those in high schools. College instructors have advanced degrees and know their subjects extremely well. High school teachers are well qualified but generally have only four-year degrees. College courses are geared toward very specific goals and last only a few months, whereas high school courses are simpler, more general, and last for the whole school term. Also, in college you are working toward a main goal, which you choose yourself. The time demands are very different. In high school the whole year is spent on five subjects and the five books to go with them, but in college twice as many books and ideas are covered in half as much time, and the student must do all the preparation on his or her own time.

1 Which sentence is the topic sentence? _____

2 What two topics are "announced" in the topic sentence?

_____

3 Does the topic sentence state that the topics will be compared

or contrasted?_____

4 How is the supporting detail arranged?_____

5 List the transition words and phrases used in the paragraph.

_____

6 When should the following transitions be inserted in the paragraph?

finally_____

for example_____

in contrast_____

the courses are also different_____

7 Which sentence seems unrelated to the rest of the paragraph?

_____

8 Can you rewrite the sentence so that it has relevant supporting

detail? _____

9 Write a good concluding sentence for this paragraph. _____

_____

7 Read the following paragraph. Underline the transitions.

College is very demanding; you must study in order to pass. You can't just go home and study overnight and pass the next day's test. I have found that the courses are much harder than the courses I had in high school; so I have learned to study more, and because of this, I have learned more and become more aware of things. High school was a totally different thing. I can remember the times I could just go home to look over a book the night before I took a test and passed it. The courses were easier, and I could get by with lower grades then, but from the moment I took the entrance exams for college, things have been different.

1 Write a good topic sentence for this paragraph. _____

_____

2 List the transition words and phrases used in the paragraph.

_____

_____

172

3 Is this paragraph organized continuously or discontinuously?

_____

4 Is there enough detail to make the paragraph interesting and well developed?

_____

8 Read the following paragraph, paying close attention to the organization of details.

   The high school student is generally young and living with his parents. The college student is more independent, living on his own and often working full- or part-time to support himself. The college student will be taking more difficult courses, and often his work may interfere with studying, whereas a high school student will have a slower pace and fewer distractions. The college student may have more specialized instructors to motivate him, however, whereas the high school student may be motivated by the more personal attention he receives from his instructors.

1 Write a topic sentence for this paragraph. _____

_____

2 Write a concluding sentence for this paragraph. _____

_____

3 How is the supporting detail arranged here, continuously or discontinuously?

_____

4 List the transitions used to link detail in this paragraph.____

_____

5 What weakness is illustrated by this paragraph? _____

_____

Readings_____

From *The Indian Heritage of America*

Alvin M. Josephy

9 The following paragraph is a sample from the essay that begins on page 176. By reading this paragraph and answering the questions, you will prepare yourself to read and understand the entire essay more easily.

Common among most whites are the false understandings and underlined images which they underlined retain about Indians. For many, the moving pictures, television, and comic strips have firmly established a stereotype as the true portrait of all Indians: the dour, stoic, warbonneted Plains Indian. He is a warrior, he has no humor unless it is that of an incongruous and farcical type, and his language is full of "hows," "ughs," and words that end in "um." Only rarely in the popular media of communications is it hinted that Indians, too, were, and are, all kinds of real, living persons like any others and that they included peace-loving wise men, mothers who cried for the safety of their children, young men who sang songs of love and courted maidens, dullards, statesmen, cowards, and patriots. Today there are college-trained Indians, researchers, business and professional men and women, jurists, ranchers, teachers and political office holders. Yet so enduring is the stereotype that many a non-Indian, especially if he lives in an area where Indians are not commonly seen, expects any American Indian he meets to wear a feathered headdress. When he sees the Indian in a conventional business suit instead, he is disappointed!

Reading for Meaning

1 Locate the underlined words in the paragraph, and reread the sentences in which they appear. Write your own definition of what the word means in that sentence. Use a dictionary if necessary.

images _____

retain _____

stereotype _____

dour _____

stoic _____

incongruous _____

farcical _____

courted _____

dullards _____

conventional _____

Reading for Structure

2 What two topics are developed in this paragraph? _____

3 Is there a topic sentence? If so, which sentence performs this

function? _____

4 What topic is developed by the details in sentences 2 and 3?

_____

5 What topic is developed by the details in sentences 4 and 5?

_____

6 What transition, if any, separates these two groups of details?

_____

7 What topic is developed by sentence 6? _____

8 What topic is developed by sentence 7? _____

9 List the transition words used in these last two sentences.

_____

10 Does this paragraph compare or contrast its two topics?

_____

11 Are the supporting details in continuous or discontinuous order?

_____

10 Now read the entire essay "From *The Indian Heritage of America*" with the sample paragraph in place.

[1] Common among most whites are the false understandings and images which they retain about Indians. For many, the moving pictures, television, and comic strips have firmly established a stereotype as the true portrait of all Indians: the dour, stoic, warbonneted Plains Indian. He is a warrior, he has no humor unless it is that of an incongruous and farcical type, and his language is full of "hows," "ughs," and words that end in "um." Only rarely in the popular media of communications is it hinted that Indians, too, were, and are, all kinds of real, living persons like any others and that they included peace-loving wise men, mothers who cried for the safety of their children, young men who sang songs of love and courted maidens, dullards, statesmen, cowards, and patriots. Today there are college-trained Indians, researchers, business and professional men and women, jurists, ranchers, teachers and political office holders. Yet so enduring is the stereotype that many a non-Indian, especially if he lives in an area where Indians are not commonly seen, expects any American Indian he meets to wear a feathered headdress. When he sees the Indian in a conventional business suit instead, he is disappointed!

[2] If Indians themselves are still about as real as wooden sticks to many non-Indians, the facts concerning their present-day status in the societies of the Americas are even less known. Again, stereotypes, like those of "the oil-rich Indian" or "the coddled ward of Uncle Sam" frequently obscure the truth. A few Indians have become wealthy, but most of them know poverty, ill health, and barren, wasted existences. Some have received higher education, but many are poorly educated or not educated at all. Some are happily assimilated in the white man's societies; others are in various stages of acculturation, and many are not assimilated and do not wish to be anything but Indian. In the United States, in addition, it often comes as a surprise to many otherwise well-informed whites to learn

176

that the Indians are citizens and have the right to vote; that reservations are not <u>concentration</u> camps but are all the lands that were left to the Indians, and that are still being guarded by them as homes from which they can come and go in freedom; that the special treaty rights that they possess and that make them a <u>unique</u> <u>minority</u> in the nation are payments and <u>guarantees</u> given them for land they sold to the non-Indian people of the United States; that Indians pay state and federal taxes like all other citizens, save where treaties, agreements, or <u>statutes</u> have <u>exempted</u> them; and that, far from being on the way to <u>extinction</u>, the Indian population is increasing rapidly.

[3] Finally, there are facts that should be obvious to everyone after five hundred years but are not, possibly because Columbus's name for them, Indians, is to this day understood by many to refer to a single people. Despite the still commonly asked question, "Do you speak Indian?" there is neither a single Indian people nor a single Indian language, but many different peoples, with different <u>racial</u> characteristics, different <u>cultures</u>, and different languages. From Alaska to Cape Horn, in fact, the Indians of the Americas are as different from each other as are Spaniards, Scots, and Poles—and, in many cases, as will be seen, they are even more different.

Reading for Meaning

1 Locate the underlined words in the essay, and reread the sentences in which they appear. Write your own definition of what the word means in that sentence. Use a dictionary if necessary.

coddled _____

ward _____

obscure _____

barren _____

assimilated _____

acculturation _____

concentration _____

unique _____

minority _____

guarantees _____

statutes _____

exempted _____

extinction _____

racial _____

cultures _____

Reading for Structure

2 Paragraph 1 is about historical stereotypes and the real Indian past. What topics are developed in paragraph 2?

_____

3 What transition is used to link paragraphs 1 and 2?

_____

4 Which sentence is the topic sentence of paragraph 2?

_____

5 What topic is developed by sentence 2 in this paragraph?

_____

6 What topic is developed by sentence 3? _____

7 What transition links sentences 2 and 3? _____

8 What topic (or topics) is developed in sentence 4? _____

_____

9 What transition links the two parts of sentence 4? _____

10 What topic (or topics) is developed in sentence 5?

_____

11 What transition words are used in sentence 5?

_____

12 What topic is developed by the last sentence? _____

13 Does this paragraph compare or contrast its two topics? ____

14 Are the supporting details in continuous or discontinuous order?

_____

15 What topics are developed in paragraph 3? _____

16 What transition introduces this paragraph? _____

17 Which of the two topics is developed at greatest length?

_____

18 Is paragraph 3 in continuous or discontinuous order? _____

Comprehension Test

19 What is the common stereotype of Indians as painted by movies, television, and comic strips? _____

_____

_____

_____

_____

179

20 What are the common misconceptions about the Indian's place in society?

_____

_____

_____

_____

21 What is the truth about the Indian's status? _____

_____

_____

_____

22 Can all Indian people be classified under the general heading

of "Indian"? Why? _____

_____

_____

23 From this essay, what are some conclusions you can draw about

American society's attitude toward the Indian? _____

_____

_____

_____

24 What is the author's attitude toward Indians? Explain.

_____

_____

_____

_____

Writing Assignments

25 Write a paragraph in which you contrast an ethnic or minority
group with their public image or stereotype.

_____

_____

_____

_____

_____

_____

_____

_____

_____

_____

_____

_____

_____

_____

_____

_____

_____

_____

_____

_____

_____

_____

_____

_____

_____

_____

_____

_____

_____

26 Write a paragraph contrasting what students are really like with what people think students are like.

_____

_____

_____

_____

_____

_____

_____

_____

_____

_____

_____

_____

_____

_____

_____

_____

_____

_____

_____

_____

_____

_____

_____

_____

_____

_____

27 Write a paragraph in which you contrast the results of treating people as they are with treating people as they ought to be. Illustrate your paragraph with examples from your own experience.

_____

_____

_____

_____

_____

_____

_____

_____

_____

_____

183

_____

_____

_____

_____

_____

_____

_____

_____

_____

_____

_____

_____

_____

_____

Readings ———————

From *The Log from the Sea of Cortez*

John Steinbeck

1 The following paragraph is a sample from the essay that begins on page 188. By reading this paragraph and answering the questions, you will prepare yourself to read and understand the entire essay more easily.

There is a strange <u>duality</u> in the human which makes for an <u>ethical paradox</u>. We have definitions of good qualities and of bad; not changing things, but generally considered good and bad throughout the ages and throughout the species. Of the good, we think always of wisdom, <u>tolerance</u>, kindliness, generosity, <u>humility</u>; and the qualities of cruelty, greed, self-interest, <u>graspingness</u>, and <u>rapacity</u> are universally considered undesirable. And yet in our structure of society, the so-called and considered good qualities are <u>invariable concomitants</u> of failure, while the bad ones are the cornerstones of success. A man—a <u>viewing-point</u> man—while he will love the <u>abstract</u> good qualities and detest the abstract bad, will nevertheless envy and admire the person who through possessing the bad qualities has succeeded economically and socially, and will hold in contempt that person whose good qualities have caused failure. When such a viewing-point man thinks of Jesus or St. Augustine or Socrates he regards them with love because they are the symbols of the good he admires, and he hates the symbols of the bad. But actually he would rather be successful than good. In an animal other than man we would replace the term "good" with "weak survival <u>quotient</u>" and the term "bad" with "strong survival quotient." Thus, man in his thinking or <u>reverie</u> status admires the <u>progression</u> toward <u>extinction</u>, but in the unthinking <u>stimulus</u> which really activates him he tends toward survival. Perhaps no other animal is so torn between alternatives. Man might be described fairly adequately, if simply, as a two-legged paradox. He has never become accustomed to the tragic miracle of consciousness. Perhaps, as has been suggested, his species is not set, has not <u>jelled</u>, but is still in a state of becoming, bound by his physical memories to a past struggle and survival, limited in his futures by the uneasiness of thought and consciousness.

Reading for Meaning

1 Locate the underlined words in the paragraph, and reread the sentences in which they appear. Write your own definition of what the word means in that sentence. Use a dictionary if necessary.

duality _____

ethical paradox _____

tolerance _____

humility _____

graspingness _____

rapacity _____

invariable concomitants _____

viewing-point _____

abstract _____

quotient _____

reverie status _____

progression _____

extinction _____

stimulus_____

jelled _____

Reading for Structure

2 What is the topic developed in this paragraph?

_____

3 Is there a topic sentence? Which sentence is the topic sentence?

_____

4 Which sentences contain supporting detail that develops the topic of human idealistic ideas about good and bad qualities?

_____

5 Which sentences describe how these good and bad qualities actually function in society?

_____

6 What transition phrase separates the two groups of supporting detail?

_____

7 Sentences 5, 6, and 7 alternately develop first the topic of human idealistic ideas of good and evil, then the human realistic approach to good and evil. Is this continuous or discontinuous organization?

_____

8 Is this comparison or contrast? _____

9 List the transition words used in sentences 5, 6, and 7 that signal this relationship to the reader.

_____

10 Sentence 8 introduces another topic. What is this topic?

_____

11 What two topics are developed in the rest of the paragraph?

_____

12 List the transitions used in sentences 8 to 13.

_____

13 Are these two topics compared or contrasted? _____

14 Is the last section of the paragraph arranged in continuous or

discontinuous order? _____

15 Which sentence is the concluding sentence? _____

_____

16 How does it sum up both the first and second sections of the

paragraph? _____

_____

12 Now read the entire essay "From *The Log from the Sea of Cortez*" with the sample paragraphs in place.

[1] It is interesting to see how areas are sometimes <u>dominated</u> by one or two species. On this beach the yellow-green cucumber was everywhere, with giant brittle-stars a close second. Neither of these animals has any <u>effective offensive property</u> as far as we know, although neither of them seems to be a <u>delicacy</u> enjoyed by other animals. There does seem to be a balance which, when passed by a certain <u>species</u>, allows that animal <u>numerically</u> to dominate a given area. When this <u>threshold</u> of successful reproduction and survival is crossed, the area becomes the special residence of this form. Then it seems other animals which might be either hostile or perhaps the prey of the dominating animal would be wiped out or would desert the given area. In many cases the arrival and success of a species seem to be by chance entirely. In some northern areas, where the ice of winter yearly <u>scours</u> and cleans the rocks, it has been noted that summer brings sometimes one <u>dominant</u> species and sometimes another, the success <u>factor</u> seeming to be prior arrival and an early start. With <u>marine fauna</u>, as with humans, <u>priority</u> and possession appear to be vastly important to survival and dominance. But sometimes it is found that the very success of an animal is its downfall. There are examples where the available food supply is so exhausted by the rapid and successful reproduction that the animal must <u>migrate</u> or die. Sometimes, also, the very by-products of the animals' own

bodies prove poisonous to a too great <u>concentration</u> of their own species.

[2] It is difficult, when watching the little beasts, not to trace human <u>parallels</u>. The greatest danger to a <u>speculative</u> biologist is <u>analogy</u>. It is a pitfall to be avoided—the industry of the bee, the economics of the ant, the <u>villainy</u> of the snake, all in human terms have given us <u>profound misconceptions</u> of the animals. But parallels are amusing if they are not taken too seriously as regards the animal in question, and are downright valuable as regards humans. The routine of changing domination is a case in point. One can think of the attached and dominant human who has captured the place, the property, and the security. He dominates his area. To protect it, he has police who know him and who are <u>dependent</u> on him for a living. He is protected by good clothing, good houses, and good food. He is protected even against illness. One would say that he is safe, that he would have many children, and that his seed would in a short time litter the world. But in his fight for dominance he has pushed out others of his species who were not so fit to dominate, and perhaps these have become wanderers, improperly clothed, ill fed, having no security and no fixed <u>base.</u> These should really perish, but the reverse seems true. The dominant human, in his security, grows soft and fearful. He spends a great part of his time in protecting himself. Far from reproducing rapidly, he has fewer children, and the ones he does have are ill protected inside themselves because so thoroughly protected from without. The lean and hungry grow strong, and the strongest of them are selected out. Having nothing to lose and all to gain, these selected hungry and <u>rapacious</u> ones develop attack rather than defense <u>techniques,</u> and become strong in them, so that one day the dominant man is <u>eliminated</u> and the strong and hungry wanderer takes his place.

[3] And the routine is repeated. The new dominant <u>entrenches</u> himself and then softens. The turnover of dominant human families is very rapid, a few generations usually <u>sufficing</u> for their rise and <u>flowering</u> and decay. Sometimes, as in the case of Hearst, the rise and glory and decay take place in one generation and nothing is left. One dominant thing sometimes does survive and that is not even well defined; some quality of the spirit of an individual continues to dominate. Whereas the great force which was Hearst has died before the death of the man and will soon be forgotten except perhaps as a <u>ridiculous</u> and <u>vulgar fable</u>, the spirit and thought of Socrates not only survive, but continue as living <u>entities</u>.

[4] There is a strange duality in the human which makes for an ethical paradox. We have definitions of good qualities and of bad; not changing things, but generally considered good and bad throughout the ages and throughout the species. Of the good, we think always of wisdom, tolerance, kindliness, generosity, humility; and the qualities of cruelty, greed, self-interest, graspingness, and rapacity are universally considered undesirable. And yet in our structure of society, the so-called and considered good qualities are invariable concomitants of failure, while the bad ones are the cornerstones of success. A man—a viewing-point man—while he will love the abstract good qualities and detest the abstract bad, will nevertheless envy and admire the person who through possessing the bad qualities has succeeded economically and socially, and will hold in contempt that person whose good qualities have caused failure. When such a viewing-point man thinks of Jesus or St. Augustine or Socrates he regards them with love because they are the symbols of the good he admires, and he hates the symbols of the bad. But actually he would rather be successful than good. In an animal other than man we would replace the term "good" with "weak survival quotient" and the term "bad" with "strong survival quotient." Thus, man in his thinking or reverie status admires the progression toward extinction, but in the unthinking stimulus which really activates him he tends toward survival. Perhaps no other animal is so torn between alternatives. Man might be described fairly adequately, if simply, as a two-legged paradox. He has never become accustomed to the tragic miracle of consciousness. Perhaps, as has been suggested, his species is not set, has not jelled, but is still in a state of becoming, bound by his physical memories to a past of struggle and survival, limited in his futures by the uneasiness of thought and consciousness.

Reading for Meaning

1 Locate the underlined words in the essay, and reread the sentences in which they appear. Write your own definition of what the word means in that sentence. Use a dictionary if necessaey.

dominated _____

effective offensive property _____

delicacy _____

190

species _____

numerically _____

threshold _____

scours _____

dominant _____

factor _____

marine fauna _____

priority _____

migrate _____

concentration _____

parallels _____

speculative _____

The words in the left-hand column are underlined in the essay.
Reread the sentences in which they appear, and pick, from the
choices at the right, the word that is closest in meaning. Circle
your answer.

analogy	comparison	relationship	dissection
industry	organization	business	diligence
villainy	intelligence	wickedness	peasantry
profound misconceptions	minor misconceptions	complete miscalculations	serious misunderstandings
dependent	reliant	trustworthy	divergent
base	contemptible	establish	foundation
rapacious	swift	predatory	trained
techniques	methods	technicalities	abilities
eliminated	expelled	ignored	entitled
entrenches	furrows	encroaches	establishes

sufficing	hardship	sufficient	competent
flowering	developing	blooming	flourishing
ridiculous	absurd	deriding	abounding
vulgar fable	obscene story	common fact	vernacular text
entities	wholeness	designations	real existences

Reading for Structure

2 What is the topic developed in paragraph 1? _____

3 Is there a topic sentence in paragraph 1? If so, which sentence

is it? _____

4 List the transitions used to introduce supporting detail in para-

graph 1. _____

5 How is the supporting detail in the first part of the paragraph

generally arranged? _____

6 Notice the transition that begins sentence 10. Do sentences 10,
11, and 12 contain information that is compared or contrasted

to the first section of the paragraph? _____

7 Which sentence functions as a transition between paragraphs

1 and 2? _____

8 What topic is developed in paragraph 2? _____

9 Is there a topic sentence in paragraph 2? _____

10 What is the function of sentences 2, 3, and 4 in paragraph 2?

_____

11 What topic is developed by the details in sentences 6 to 11 in this paragraph? _____

12 What topic is developed in sentences 12 and 13 in paragraph 2?

_____

13 What transition word separates these two groups of detail?

_____

14 What topic is developed in sentences 14, 15, and 16? _____

15 What topic is developed in sentences 17 and 18? _____

16 Is there a transition separating sentences 14 to 16 from sentences 17 and 18? Why? _____

17 Is paragraph 2 arranged continuously or discontinuously?

_____

18 Is paragraph 2 a comparison or a contrast paragraph? _____

19 What two topics are contrasted in paragraph 3? _____

20 What transition word introduces this contrast? _____

21 What is the function of paragraph 3? _____

22 What is the relationship between paragraph 1 and paragraphs 2, 3, and 4? _____

23 Are the paragraphs in this essay arranged continuously or discontinuously? _____

Comprehension Test

24 Name the two most plentiful animals found on the beach.

_____

_____

25 Why were these two the most plentiful? _____

_____

_____

26 What are the two most important factors in the theory of area domination?

_____

27 Why is the successful domination of an area sometimes the

downfall of the dominant species? _____

_____

_____

28 Which three animals has man consistently misunderstood?

Why? _____

_____

_____

_____

29 Listed below are the five steps in what Steinbeck calls the "routine of changing domination." Put these steps in order by placing numbers in the blanks by each statement.

_____ the weaker animals attack the dominant animals
_____ the dominant animals grow weak
_____ the weaker animals become dominant

_____ the weaker animals grow strong

_____ a certain species of animals dominates an area

30 How does it work in man? _____

_____

_____

_____

31 According to the essay, why was the Hearst family unique in its

pattern of "changing domination"? _____

_____

_____

32 What five qualities does man consider ethically good? _____

_____

33 What five qualities does man consider ethically bad? _____

_____

34 How is man's concept of good and bad opposite from that of the
animal world?

_____

_____

_____

35 Judging by the tone of the essay, what do you think is Stein-

beck's attitude toward society? _____

_____

_____

_____

_____

36 What is the main idea of the essay? Explain. _____

_____

_____

_____

_____

_____

_____

Writing Assignments

37 Write a paragraph comparing human beings to some animal (ant, bee, fox, bear, and so on).

_____

_____

_____

_____

_____

_____

_____

_____

_____

_____

_____

_____

_____

_____

_____

_____

_____

_____

_____

_____

_____

_____

38 Write a paragraph explaining to an older relation the difference between being "moral" and being "square."

_____

_____

_____

_____

_____

_____

_____

_____

_____

_____

_____

_____

_____

_____

_____

_____

_____

_____

_____

_____

_____

_____

_____

Readings _____

The Big Car Race
Jack Ludwig

3 The following paragraphs are samples from the essay that begins on page 201. By reading these paragraphs and answering the questions, you will prepare yourself to read and understand the entire essay more easily.

In Louisville only the Avis girls, off the track, dressed like jockeys; in Indianapolis during "500" week almost everybody, including sportswriters, wore a <u>crested</u> cap, a crested jacket, or any other crested thing in order to look like a racing pro. Husband and wife "teams" wandered the Speedway Museum in twin nylon jackets <u>slashed</u> with racing strips. One woman balanced an astronaut's <u>scrambled-egg</u> longpeaked cap on top of her pink plastic curlers; her jeweled prescription <u>bifocals</u> were shaped to <u>simulate</u> a driver's. Her husband wore the same cap tipped forward over aviator sunglasses gleaming with military metal. White socks <u>gaping</u> between his race-driver shoes and too-short nylon trousers were, however, <u>reassuringly</u> civilian.

In Louisville the Churchill Downs red rose—on a card, a sign, a program—was usually small and delicate (the Kentucky Derby was as frequently represented by the track's twin <u>spires</u>); in Indianapolis the "500" crossed white and checkered flags were everywhere, in all sizes. Sponsor decals that covered almost every inch of a "500" car also covered the jackets of fans, collectors, and <u>imitators</u>—oil crests, tire crests, gas crests, valve crests, battery crests, piston crests, ring crests, shock absorber crests, windshield-wiper crests were set in a <u>scatter</u> of U.S.A. and white-and-checkered flags.

Reading for Meaning

1 Locate the underlined words in the paragraph, and reread the sentences in which they appear. Write your own definition of what the word means in that sentence. Use a dictionary if necessary.

199

crested _____

slashed _____

scrambled-egg _____

bifocals _____

simulate _____

gaping _____

reassuringly _____

spires _____

imitators _____

scatter _____

Reading for Structure

2 What is the topic developed in paragraph 1? _____

3 Which is the topic sentence? _____

4 Are the Indianapolis 500 and the Kentucky Derby compared or

contrasted in this paragraph? _____

5 Which is the topic sentence in paragraph 2? _____

6 What topic is developed in this paragraph? _____

7 Is the detail in these two paragraphs organized continuously or

discontinuously? _____

8 If these were the two opening paragraphs of an essay, what do
you predict the subject(s) of that essay would be? What would
be the probable arrangement of the detail in the essay?

_____

200

Of the two subjects, the Indianapolis 500 and the Kentucky Derby, which do you think is the central subject, the one the writer will emphasize most? _____

14 Now read the entire essay "The Big Car Race" with the sample paragraphs in place.

[1] In Louisville only the Avis girls, off the track, dressed like jockeys; in Indianapolis during "500" week almost everybody, including sportswriters, wore a crested cap, a crested jacket, or any other crested thing in order to look like a racing pro. Husband and wife "teams" wandered the Speedway Museum in twin nylon jackets slashed with racing stripes. One woman balanced an astronaut's scrambled-egg longpeaked cap on top of her plastic curlers; her jeweled prescription bifocals were shaped to simulate a driver's. Her husband wore the same cap tipped forward over aviator sunglasses gleaming with military metal. White socks gaping between his race-driver shoes and too-short nylon trousers were, however, reassuringly civilian.

[2] In Louisville the Churchill Downs red rose—on a card, a sign, a program—was usually small and delicate (the Kentucky Derby was as frequently represented by the track's twin spires); in Indianapolis the "500" crossed white and checkered flags were everywhere, in all sizes. Sponsor decals that covered almost every inch of a "500" car also covered the jackets of fans, collectors and imitators—oil crests, tire crests, gas crests, valve crests, battery crests, piston crests, ring crests, shock absorber crests, windshield-wiper crests were set in a scatter of U.S.A. and white-and-checkered flags.

[3] That white-and-checkered flag <u>motif</u> showed up on bracelets, earrings, cigarette cases, lighters, crucifixes, panties, brooches, cufflinks. High on the Indianapolis petty porn scale was a peek-a-boo bra with one cup white, the other checkered —cut out where it counts, <u>ostensibly</u> to give the wearer racing room.

[4] Checkered flags, white flags as pennants, triangles, oil-cloth and plastic tatters fluttered from strung wire and clothes-line. Flags decorated gas stations, auto shops, garages, supermarkets, mobile homes, hamburger shacks, bicycle banana seats, motorcycle handlebars, car aerials. Department stores stocked checkered shirts, trousers, skirts, nightshirts, boxer shorts, swimsuits, sportscoats, which, when sold, were packed in checkered paperbags or checkered boxes and carried

in checkered shopping-bags. Checkered flags substituted for the more accurate plaque "X" to mark disaster stations pushing the usual Spectacular wares—"rooms," "eats," "parking."

[5] Car racing fans, a special breed, wear racing gloves as genuine (and expensive) as Bobby Unser's, carry hundred-buck stopwatches, hundred-buck binoculars, multihundred-buck cameras they aim at anything in decals and crests. Stopwatches, like racing caps and jackets, express the professional status of spectators. The more expensive the stopwatch, the more profoundly knowing the fan. Before the Speedway tower minisecond electronic timing device was built, the stopwatch could have been considered an _essential_ part of "500" spectatoring. The stopwatch, however, means more than its function. It supposedly stands as status, emblem, token, _fetish_, fraternity pin. The racing _aficionado_ doesn't want you to think he's just one more lousy tourist or dumb sports fan. The measure of who he is resides with his stopwatch.

[6] That stopwatch has another function. It is the staple of _trivia_ collection. A "500" aficionado speaks in 1/1000 second _differentiations_. A horse racing "in" man ticks off only one fifths. At the Kentucky Derby early morning workouts those carrying stopwatches will be track clockers, handicappers, _turfwriters_, trainers, owners, jockeys, and perhaps a very few fans. At the time trials for the Indianapolis "500" almost everyone carries some kind of stopwatch. It's a standard Christmas or birthday present in Indianapolis—kids get them for graduation, for their Bar Mitzvah. One can guess at the status, age, or "betterment" index of a stopwatch-carrier by checking out the price of the timepiece. Some people collect stopwatches. Some keep the watches they replace so that the full run becomes a personal stopwatch museum. At the time trials the overwhelming majority of those doing the timing have nothing whatsoever to do with the race. The stopwatch is the recognized local symbol of true "500" participation.

[7] Fans rate their success as "participants" not by the usual gauges alone—autographs, signed pictures, noncommercial souvenirs—but by how deeply they penetrate the Dantesque inner reaches of Gasoline Alley (where racing cars are worked on and stored). One may, on special days, buy tickets or otherwise get them, so that gawking and peeking become _legitimate_. Points are scored whenever one penetrates an _impenetrable_ barrier, or passes beyond a _proscribed_ gate; high standing is awarded anyone whose camera focused on the dark _recesses_ of a stripped-down engine. The different colored tags and badges which allow closer and closer _access_ on Race Day are soon

known, quickly recognized, greatly admired, envied, yearned for, and, sometimes, "rented," borrowed, or snatched. A commercial, industrial, or financial enterprise using the "500" to reward its employees can't simply follow its Kentucky Derby model—transport 'em, house 'em, feed 'em, amuse 'em, booze 'em. Businesses must deliver those <u>acknowledgedly</u> hard-to-come-by ribbons and badges to differentiate those *they* are rewarding. Tire companies compete with oil companies *and* with other tire companies to see who can—officially or unofficially—open the closed-off professional car racing world to those who will talk up the "500" experience the rest of their lives.

[8] In Indianapolis the code slogan is not only "I was there," but "I was almost a part of it." Pacific-8 Conference or Big Ten alumni at the Rose Bowl may identify with alma mater's doing-or-dying, yet recognize the obvious distinction between doer and watcher. Indianapolis sets the aficionado up in a special <u>limbo</u> somewhere in between. As the cop who directs traffic may develop the delusion that his wave powers cars, so the aficionado may come to believe that without his or her presence the "500" could never get started.

[9] There's also a Guinness *Book of Records* <u>mania</u> that works in Indianapolis as it does in Churchill Downs: "This is my fiftieth consecutive Derby," one is told, and proudly. Tradition is even more important than statistics trivia: an old gentleman told me he "started comin' to the '500' when I was five 'cause my daddy was a car man. Sooner missed m'own weddin' than the Race."

[10] Nobody, in my own experience at Louisville, trotted up to Churchill Downs on a horse got up to look like a Derby entry; in Indianapolis people play "pretend '500'" Their cars carry "STP" decals plastered over everything, and frequently are fitted with supplyhouse gadgets and "extras" that make every Middle American's car his chariot. Dragsters with the ass end of their Fords flipped up power their extra-wide extra-heavy whitewalls out of hidden driveways into the <u>gaggles</u> of Speedway traffic rpm-ing through Indianapolis at two miles per hour.

[11] In Indianapolis a portion of the "500" crowd looked like sidemen to Bill Haley's Comets, or Sha-Na-Na (with no put on). The 1970s duck-tailed haircut was modified long, but sharp shaped sideburns still marked the in-crowd as members of the Elvis society. Tattoos were rare in Louisville, plentiful in Indianapolis—only 100 miles away. On the interstates around Indianapolis "racers" tried out their "500" <u>strategies</u>—riding the draft, slingshotting, tailgating on the straightaways, gunning

for the inside lane, circling the field on the outside. Mufflers were considered sissy, but even mufflerless cars scutcheoned a full set of muffler-manufacturer's decals.

[12] On the Speedway approaches during trial days or Race Day democracy prevails: jalops, limousines, sportscars, campers, trailers, sandbuggies, antique cars, buses, cabs, cop cars, trapped ambulances, hemmed-in fire equipment, tow cars, "rescue units." In this unprogrammed chance parade, motorized pimps and camper-housed hookers frequently draw alongside their prospective driver-goggle-wearing Johns determinedly respectable next to their driver-goggle-wearing wives.

[13] Twenty-four hours before the big race, the great American spectacular of misrule begins—for outsiders. The "500" for Indianapolis residents means something totally different—a wonderful local holiday, the best picnic of the year, the week everybody seems cheerful and excited. For children, the "500" means fun and a change in who or what is in town. Kids in Indianapolis take up a watch on the streets that continue US or Interstate highways through the city and see if they can spot license plates from all fifty states and all the Canadian provinces. Children cover their tricycles and bicycles with "STP" decals and careen over the sidewalks, making their own soundtrack. Toy "500" cars are crashed, slammed, hurled over imaginary tracks. Slot-car play gets wild. Motorcyclists on only two wheels feel only half there Race Week. Time has to be ticked off in 1/1000th seconds all week long in order to penetrate Race consciousness.

[14] In contrast to the posh Kentucky Derby party of Mrs. C. V. Whitney was the democratic "500" Festival Queen's Ball held at the new Indiana Convention—Exposition Center. The Center was suitably decorated with 7,400 square yards of black and white checkered carpet, according to a *Star* team of reporters who further described the decor thus:

> Rising 12 feet above the tables were shimmery metal "fountains" kept in graceful motion by air currents. In the base of each flickered white votive candles, and tiny electric lights twinkled in silverleaf arches bordering the dance floor.

The reporters added reassuringly that "no 'hot pants' were in evidence," a fact Eugenia Sheppard thought not worth a mention at Mrs. Whitney's Derby party. "Several Orient-influenced gowns" and a woman with "diamond-studded eyelashes drew many comments" according to the *Star.* John Walsh, vice-president of the Indiana National Bank, appeared in a "display of honorary medals—the Order of the Tower, Indiana Society Medal and the Indiana University Medal." Not at the Queen's Ball, and not in the "500" parade because "technically it wasn't a float," was Miss Cronin's most obvious rival, "a 12-foot-high motorized Schlitz beer can [that] honked at <u>incredulous</u> spectators from a parking lot at Pennsylvania and Michigan streets."

[15] More restricted than the Queen's Ball was the Borg-Warner Corporation party at the Indiana National Bank Auditorium on Race eve, at which "most of the 350 guests roamed the terraces where the breeze was gentle and checkered flags in flower beds snapped smartly at attention." The *Star's* reporters remarked how "Indianapolis society leaders wearing safe, neat business suits and their wives" came up against the "race crowd who were wearing some pretty jazzy outfits." More exclusive yet was a party at the Columbia Club given by Mrs. Roscoe Turner for 160 guests and featuring as stars bandleader Stan Kenton and Dr. Denton Cooley, the Houston heart specialist. The *Star* also reported four formal weddings on Race eve. The big "Concerning Women" item announced that Dolly Coles, wife of the president and chief operations officer of General Motors Corporation, would be the very first woman ever to ride in an Indianapolis "500" pace car:

> Dolly had evidently told her good friend Tony Hulman, bossman of the "500," "One of these days women's liberation will get to the Speedway. When you pick the first woman to ride in the pace car on race day, please think of me." He did.

[16] In its early days the "500" made a one-to-one connection with car design and motor design. Cars in the 1970s, doing 190 miles per hour, and getting about 1.8 miles per gallon, however, aren't close relatives of the family automobile. The one familiar, and in 1972 still active, car name in racing was Ford—but only as an engine builder. Eagle, McLaren, Parnelli, Brabham, Antares, Brawner, among others, the important names in chassis design, are not very concerned about the family car.

[17] Yet, no matter how intricate the "500" engine and chassis have become, a spectator can still feel that a car is a car is a car. In Louisville, only professional racing people master the <u>genealogical intricacies</u> of horse breeding, but in Indianapolis most veteran "500" fans know a great deal about engines, <u>aerodynamic</u> principles, fuels. The Speedway Museum encourages fans to view old racing cars historically. Material is provided to explain changes in engine and chassis design during the sixty years of the "500."

[18] The horse can't be claimed as something exclusively

American; the automobile, from the point of view of the "500" fan, is. The Indianapolis Speedway Museum is an American repository of technological history and social nostalgia. The "500" has always been something American, unlike the Grand Prix, whose cars and drivers have been, for the most part, foreign.

[19] Sports car races are considered foreign, too, and worse —uppity. In the 1972 "500" a sports car racer, Sam Posey, was driving a big "500" car as an outsider and interloper. The late Peter Revson, Grand Prix in character, sports car in social class, wasn't accepted as true "500." Stock car drivers like southerner Cale Yarborough fit the Indianapolis image better than the Poseys and the Revsons, who, Middle America feels, are only slumming in Indianapolis.

[20] No other spectacular is so closely identified with one level of American society as the Indianapolis "500," yet Middle America does not control the big car race. Just as the Kentucky Derby higher society enclaves are sealed off from the masses, so, too, are Indianapolis's. The "Paddock" section and penthouse seats reflect one's Indianapolis social standing: there one sees few racing caps and almost no racing jackets. Indianapolis society dresses in sports clothes little different from what's worn at the Kentucky Derby several weeks earlier.

[21] Race rituals resemble Derby rituals—"club" breakfasts, for example, which are followed by travel on buses assigned VIP traffic lanes. Club members do a lot of hard drinking in the morning, afternoon, and night of the race: Kentucky Bourbon and branch water in Indianapolis demonstrate cultural exchange.

[22] Once on the ground, the Paddock people made their way back to the buses privileged to travel those designated clear lanes. Everyone quickly changed into party clothes. Post-race parties were exciting because the winners of the better pools were declared—as the climax to the thirty-five or forty-hour party that began Race eve.

[23] For some people, though, the "500" was a five-day blow, or six, or seven. Those *outside* thought the real fun was the infield *inside,* but "500" parties, celebrations, dances, hops, gigs, funkies, formals, smoke-ins, sniff-ins, freak-outs went on all over Indianapolis. The race people—drivers, crews, owners, —constituted one important "500" group, sometimes joined by the media and other "500" public relations extensions. Sponsors, equipment manufacturers, bankers, local and national financial, industrial, and business people shared the action, too.

[24] In Louisville, though Kentuckians were prominent, the real "stars," as I've indicated, were, on the whole, outsiders. In Indianapolis, stars were rare and, for the most part, local. The "500" belongs to the city of Indianapolis and, by hospitable extension, to the rest of Indiana; the Kentucky Derby exists for Kentucky and the entire nation—and also for Louisville. The horse set establishes the Derby's tone and has no exact parallel in the Indianapolis power structure. In place of "addresses," finishing, prep, and Ivy schools, Indianapolis seems to value business affiliation. Society pages don't cater to the old-hat eastern social hierarchy. Business hierarchy is what matters. Star status is conferred by position in a firm's power structure. Locally based but nationally known firms score highest. Next come national organizations with a thriving branch or division in Indianapolis or elsewhere in Indiana. In Indianapolis society pages, board chairmen rank above presidents, presidents outrank vice-presidents, and so on right down the corporate foot-nichery, a system familiar, say, to readers of *Fortune.*

[25] Indianapolis also seems free of upwomanship in designer clothes or gourmet cookery. Few, if any, Halstons, Norells, Diors, Coco Chanels, or even Bonnie Cashins show up. At the big Borg-Warner party, the hostess—the president's wife—was refreshingly described as wearing "a long dress of crisp white pique ... scroll-edged with cotton plaid," no fashion-show stopper. She said her plaid "has no meaning. I don't even know the name of the tartan, but I like the dress."

[26] The food at this same party was characteristically local: the guests "sampled breasts, beef tenderloin, smoked salom [*sic*], chicken wings, roast diced duck in orange sauce, and imported cheeses." No cuisine starred items to invoke the great names of the "500"—Ralph DePalma *boeuf cordon bleu,* for instance, or Pete DePaolo *canard roti,* Wilbur Shaw *Petits fours,* Mauri Rose *napoleon.* Unlike Mrs. C. V. Whitney at the Derby, the star "500" hostess hadn't just rushed back from Spain or anywhere else foreign. She was from Indiana; her two sons weren't given the eastern education Fitzgerald's St. Paul considered essential. Both attended Indiana University.

[27] Four couples married the night before the "500" rated bride pictures in the Race Day *Star.* Every college or university affiliation mentioned was local or Indiana—I.U., Purdue, Indiana Central College, Butler University, or Indiana-Purdue (the last three located right in Indianapolis). No space was assigned to describe the bride's dress. The only information beyond name, parentage, and university/college affiliation considered

important was honeymoon destination. Three of the couples chose St. Louis, the Smokies, French Lick; the fourth declined to say. For all, the future home address given was Indianapolis.

[28] Down the imaginary social scale, "foreign" intrusion became even less significant. The "500," like Mardi Gras, is, as I've already suggested, a great *local* holiday. Those who come to the "500" from all over the country and the world don't really affect the "500" 's essentially local flavor. The masses who wear the checkered-flag insignia identify totally with the "home" side.

[29] In the infield and in the forty-acre "fun field" the usual Spectacular-followers were doing the usual Fort Lauderdale things, but the largest number of Fort Lauderdale jocks were from Indiana or attended Indiana universities. Sweatshirts and T-shirts parodied "Virginia is for lovers" into "Indiana is for lovers" or advertised certain Indiana institutions—Valparaiso Tech, West Baden College, Ball State, Hanover College, Huntington College; slightly better-known places such as Earlham College, De Pauw, Butler; nationally recognized Indiana University, Purdue, Notre Dame. The "500" provided an opportunity for one *to be* Fort Lauderdale without having to travel *to* Fort Lauderdale (or, that is, to leave Indiana).

[30] Without a computer or scientific head-count, I guessed that beer and wine drinkers outnumbered potsmokers better than 100–1 in Indianapolis—and only 10–1 in Louisville. Indianapolis drunks, in decibel competition with "500" engines, seemed to yowl much more loudly than Louisville drunks. Non-stop chugalug had its predictable consequences: almost cheerfully, infielders threw up a lot, zonked out a lot, or clung blearily to a car hood, a tree, fence, pole, or each other. From Lousville through New Orleans, people rushed to get to a spectacular in order to drink, smoke, or seconal themselves into instant oblivion. A significant portion of the "500" infield population missed the 1972 race: many in that group did not come to Indianapolis to see a race.

[31] People attend the spectaculars to be where the action is. I don't refer to the obvious participating pickpockets, panhandlers, proselyters, palmists, policemen, politicians, plugolas, potsellers, padres, pacifists, paramours, pariahs, parsons, prostitutes, patrons, pigeons, pedants, pushers, peekers, pentecostals, pimps, prestidigitators, prophets, punks, prudes, prattlers. Lousiville, or Indianapolis, or Miami Beach, or New Orleans—if not Pasadena—is "where it's happening." The attendant circuses make the spectacular event almost secondary because

the spectacular creates an instant community of <u>festive</u> misrule.

[32] Indianapolis is a populist phenomenon, a spectacular
which seems free of hierarchy and a ruling <u>elite.</u> Middle America is at home in Indianapolis 365 days a year: the "500" is a
Memorial Day celebration of Middle America's being "back
home."

Reading for Meaning

1 Locate the underlined words in the essay, and reread the sentences in which they appear. Write your own definition of what
the word means in that sentence. Use a dictionary if necessary.

motif _____

ostensibly _____

essential _____

fetish _____

aficionado _____

trivia _____

differentiations _____

turfwriters _____

legitimate _____

impenetrable _____

proscribed _____

recesses _____

access _____

acknowledgedly _____

limbo _____

The words in the left-hand column are underlined in the essay.
Reread the sentences in which they appear, and pick, from the
choices at the right, the word that is closest in meaning. Circle
your answer.

mania	lunacy	craze	fanaticism
gaggles	numerous	chokes	lines
strategies	policies	plans	designs
scutcheoned	displayed	utilized	obtained
prevails	triumphs	persists	predominates
determinedly	firmly	resolving	deciding
misrule	tyranny	disorder	avoidance
provinces	businesses	sections	spheres
careen	lurch	tilt	ride madly
consciousness	awakeness	scrupulousness	awareness
posh	unorganized	private	glamorous
decor	ornaments	interior decorations	orderliness
votive	offering	selective	substantive
incredulous	dishonest	skeptical	disbelieving
genealogical	history	lineage	nonspecific
intricacies	machinations	complications	analyses
aerodynamic	wind resistances	space travel	plane technology
repository	censure	quiet place	storage place
nostalgia	memorabilia	panacea	queasiness
interloper	invader	intruder	introvert
enclaves	racial distinctions	territorial distinctions	cultural distinctions
constituted	formed	established	fixed
extensions	compasses	outgrowths	connections

affiliation	kinship	association	attraction
pique	fabric	irritation	provocation
salom [*sic*]	beef	fish	pork
cuisine	cooking	kitchen	menu
proselyters	speakers	fiction writers	converters
paramours	illicit lovers	borders	deviates
pariahs	prairie dogs	outcasts	priests
pedants	teachers	show-offs	flags
pentecostals	Canadians	salesmen	religious persons
prestidigitators	adventurers	sleight-of-hand artists	social climbers
festive	sore	happy	sad
elite	controlling group	choice part	superior group

Reading for Structure

2 Which sentence is the topic sentence in paragraph 6?

_____

3 What topics are compared or contrasted in paragraph 6?

_____

4 Which details develop the function of stopwatches at Churchill Downs?

_____

5 What transition links these two sentences?

_____

6 What transition reintroduces details about the Indianapolis "500"?

_____

7 What does "it" represent in sentence 7? _____

8 Which is the concluding sentence in paragraph 6?

_____

9 Is this paragraph arranged continuously or discontinuously?

_____

10 What topic is developed in paragraph 8? _____

11 Is there a topic sentence in paragraph 8? Which sentence is the

topic sentence? _____

12 What other topics are developed in this paragraph? Are they

compared or contrasted? _____

13 What topics are contrasted in paragraph 10? _____

_____

14 Which is the topic sentence in paragraph 10?

_____

15 What is the topic developed in paragraph 11? _____

16 Which detail develops the contrasted topic—the crowd at the

Kentucky Derby? _____

17 The last few details in paragraph 11 return to description of the
fans' automobiles. Could paragraphs 11 and 12 be made one

long paragraph? Why? _____

18 Which is the topic sentence in paragraph 14? _____

_____

19 What transition is used to introduce the contrasting topic in

paragraph 14? _____

20 What transition links the topics of paragraphs 14 and 15?

_____

21 In paragraph 17, what transition is used to introduce the details

about horse racing? _____

22 What transition is used to introduce supporting detail about

auto racing in paragraph 17? _____

23 Paragraph 19 contrasts fans' attitudes toward sports car drivers
and stock car drivers. What sentence functions as a transition
to this paragraph, linking it and the paragraphs contrasting

auto racing and horse racing? _____

_____

24 In paragraphs 19 and 20, what topics are developed? _____

_____

25 Are these topics compared or contrasted? _____

26 Is the arrangement of detail continuous or discontinuous in
these two paragraphs?

_____

27 Which sentence is the topic sentence for both paragraphs?

_____

28 Which is the topic sentence in paragraph 24? Are there one or

two topic sentences? _____

_____

29 Is paragraph 24 arranged continuously or discontinuously?

_____

Comprehension Test

30 Describe the dress at Indianapolis during "500" week.

_____

31 What kinds of crests are worn on the jackets?

_____

32 What two emblems symbolize the horse racing at Louisville?

_____

33 Name four things the white and checkered flag appears on at "Indy."

_____

34 How do the commercial establishments in Indy "cash in" on

the use of the white-and-checkered flag? _____

_____

35 What is the most important item a serious race fan carries? Why?

_____

36 What is gasoline alley? Why is it important to fans?

_____

37 What is the difference between a "company" trip to Indianapo-

lis and one to Louisville? _____

_____

38 What is "Guinness _Book of Records_ mania?"

_____

39 Describe the automobiles of the Indy audience.

_____

40 What is the "500" like for people who live in Indianapolis?

_____

41 Describe the "500" Festival Parade.

_____

42 Describe the Queen's Ball.

_____

43 Name two other parties held for the "500." How do they differ

from the Queen's Ball? _____

_____

44 Which of the major car makers in America were still active in

Indy racing in 1972? What did they build? _____

_____

45 Why is the "500" considered exclusively American?

_____

46 What is the "Paddock" section at Indy?

_____

47 What are some of the differences in "tone" between the Indy
"500" and the Kentucky Derby?

_____

48 Contrast the foods served at the Indy "500" and the Kentucky

Derby. _____

_____

49 What is the author's major point in this essay? _____

_____

50 What is the author's attitude toward his subject?

_____

51 List five comparisons or contrasts between specific features of the Indy "500" and the Kentucky Derby.

_____

_____

_____

_____

Writing Assignments

52 Write a paragraph comparing or contrasting two sports with which you are familiar.

_____

_____

_____

_____

_____

_____

_____

_____

_____

_____

_____

_____

_____

_____

_____

_____

_____

_____

_____

_____

_____

_____

53 Write a paragraph in which you compare or contrast the crowds who attend two types of sports "spectaculars" with which you are familiar.

_____

_____

_____

_____

_____

_____

_____

_____

_____

_____

_____

_____

_____

_____

_____

_____

_____

_____

54 Contrast a good weekend with a bad one. For this paragraph, choose supporting details to emphasize your feelings about these two weekends.

_____

_____

_____

_____

_____

_____

_____

_____

_____

_____

_____

_____

_____

_____

_____

_____

_____

_____

_____

_____

_____

_____

5 The Organization of Essays

The first four chapters of this book focused on reading and understanding the organization of paragraphs. Paragraphs, because they are short, make good subjects for reading and writing exercises, but the essay—composed, of course, of paragraphs—is the most common form of writing or reading assignment.

Essentially, the organization of an essay is very similar to the organization of paragraphs, which you already know. In fact, it is tempting to think of an essay as a larger, expanded paragraph, for the most important difference between these two forms is that the essay has a broader subject and, because of this, the essay requires a great deal more detail to illustrate, develop, or prove its main ideas.

The Beginning. Just as a paragraph begins with a topic sentence to announce its subject and the central idea, an essay usually begins with a *thesis sentence.* A thesis sentence announces the subject of the entire essay, and generally it also makes an assertion about that subject. A very long essay may begin with an anecdote, some statistics, or a bit of background that will help the reader understand the subject of the essay, but this is sometimes omitted. In fact, the thesis sentence itself, very much like the topic sentence, may be omitted altogether; or it may appear later, particularly in a longer essay.

The Body or Development Paragraphs. Just as a paragraph's topic sentence requires detail to illustrate or develop its points, so does a thesis sentence require detail. However, a paragraph is developed by its main supporting ideas and details contained in a few sentences; an essay has a *body* or *development paragraph* devoted to each of its supporting ideas. These development paragraphs must be arranged, just as supporting sentences in a paragraph are arranged, by one of the principles of arrangement that you already know: comparison-contrast, spatial, chronological, or general-to-specific order. Transitions are sometimes used at the beginning or end of a paragraph to signal this arrangement to the reader. In addition to the order *between* paragraphs, all the principles for organization which you have learned still apply *within* each development paragraph. So an essay is organized on at least two levels: within each paragraph itself and within the larger framework of the essay.

The Ending. Many essays have a separate conclusion paragraph (or sometimes more than one), which follows the development paragraphs. By repeating key words, using synonyms for the central ideas, or using pronouns to refer to central characters or ideas, the conclusion paragraph, like the conclusion sentence, "sums up" and restates the main idea of the essay. Occasionally, a conclusion paragraph will end with a quotation, another short narrative or anecdote, or, if the subject is controversial or current, with a "call to action," which asks that the reader change his or her attitudes or begin some task the author has in mind.

Compare these outlines of both an essay and a paragraph. Notice the parallel arrangements of the elements in each of the forms. Each element of the paragraph, which you already know, has its counterpart in the organization of the essay.

The Essay

I. Introductory Paragraph
   A. Background Information
   B. Thesis Sentence

II. Body Paragraph #1
   A. Topic Sentence
   B. Major Supporting Detail #1
   C. Major Supporting Detail #2
   D. Major Supporting Detail #3

III. Body Paragraph #2
   A. Topic Sentence
   B. Major Supporting Detail #1

The Paragraph

I. Body Paragraph
   A. Topic Sentence
   B. Major Supporting Detail #1
   C. Major Supporting Detail #2

221

    C. Major Supporting
       Detail #2
    D. Major Supporting
       Detail #3

       D. Major Supporting
          Detail #3
       E. Conclusion Sentence

IV. Body Paragraph #3
    A. Topic Sentence
    B. Major Supporting
       Detail #1
    C. Major Supporting
       Detail #2
    D. Major Supporting
       Detail #3

V. Conclusion
    A. Restatement and
       Summary
    B. Quotation or
       Anecdote

1 Read the following paragraph. Underline the supporting details.

   My criteria for evaluating an instructor are the teacher's interest in his subject, the teacher's respect for his students, and the teacher's knowledge of the subjects that he is teaching. First, a teacher has to be interested in a subject to make it interesting to his students. Second, I think a teacher has to respect his students. After all, a college student does not like to be treated like a junior high school student. Most importantly, a teacher has to be knowledgeable in the subject that he teaches.

1 What topic is developed in this paragraph?_____

2 List the three major supporting details used to develop this topic._____

_____

3 What principle of arrangement is used to order these details?

_____

_____

_____

_____

2 Now read the paragraph with added detail, expanded into an essay on the same subject.

My criteria for evaluating a teacher are the teacher's interest in his subject, the teacher's respect for his students, and the teacher's knowledge of the subjects that he is teaching. It takes all these qualities to teach effectively.

A teacher has to be interested in a subject to make it interesting to his students. I once had a teacher who disliked a subject so much that he would stand four to five feet away from his notes. He told us at the beginning of the quarter that he disliked the course and through the rest of the quarter he eventually won the whole class over to his opinion. If this teacher had shown some interest in the subject, his students would have done better work.

I think a teacher has to respect his students. After all, a college student does not like to be treated like a junior high school student. A teacher has to give a student's ideas credit, or he will make that student think less of his own creative thinking. If a teacher is constantly ridiculing a student's ideas, the student will become discouraged and sometimes give up.

Most importantly, a teacher has to be knowledgeable in the subject that he teaches. If a teacher shows that he knows only enough to give a scant outline of the subject, then the students will only study enough to learn a scant outline of a course. This is only natural.

A teacher is the most important part of a subject. He guides the student through the subject. If he doesn't have these three virtues—interest, respect, knowledge—he cannot be a good teacher.

1 What topic is developed in this essay? _____

2 How is this topic subdivided? List the three parts. _____

_____

3 What topic is developed in paragraph 2? _____

4 How is this topic developed? _____

5 Which sentence is the topic sentence? _____

_____

6 Which is the topic sentence in paragraph 3? _____

_____

7 Which is the topic sentence in paragraph 4? _____

_____

8 What transition introduces the topic of paragraph 4? _____

9 What is the function of paragraph 5? _____

10 What is the principle of arrangement used in this essay?

_____

11 Which words in the last paragraph have been repeated

throughout the essay? _____

_____

3 Now read this essay on the same subject. Underline the topic sentence of each paragraph as you read.

In the evaluation of a teacher, several standards and characteristics of that teacher have to be considered, such as adaptability, preparation, and the ability to inspire respect.

Of great importance is that a teacher should be adaptable. Changing situations, unplanned-for conflicts, and cancellations could shake a teacher; but a good teacher should be ready to adapt to the new situations, to settle the conflicts or compensate for them, and to have materials and different classroom techniques that can be used when a film or program has been canceled. This teacher feels comfortable when around the students and conveys to them a feeling of security. No matter what may be the problem, the teacher has control, but the control is not so complete that creativity is impaired. The teacher has the ability to communicate, and he gives the students opportunities to find outlets for their creative drives. The teacher knows when to encourage the students while at the same time he knows when to stop and let the students handle their own capabilities.

Is the teacher well prepared and efficient? One block to a student's ability to learn is certainly the way a teacher presents his lessons. Students know when a teacher is not well prepared.

This situation gives the class an awkward atmosphere; the teacher has let himself down on the student's level, and, with this, the teacher has lost respect.

Many teachers have problems with being good advisors and friends to the students and maintaining the teacher-student relationship. A teacher should be trustworthy, considerate, and friendly but should not let this interfere with the effectiveness of his teaching. There has to be a stopping point, or the students will think of the teacher as a "good guy." The respect that is necessary for a teacher can easily be lost. Then, no matter how adaptable a teacher or efficient the method of teaching, the students do not have the right conception and frame of mind to learn. Even a teacher's appearance can alter a student's respect for him.

But the greatest impression to be made is made when all three qualities are present, and the students realize that the teacher is serious and that he really enjoys his work. The most effective teacher is the one who tries and succeeds in getting his students to understand and enjoy learning. He makes the students grateful for the educative process, and, in return, the students are determined to strive for more knowledge.

1 Which sentence announces the subject of the entire essay?

_____

2 What are the topics of the body paragraphs? _____

_____

3 Are there topic sentences in paragraphs 2, 3, and 4? _____

4 What principle is used to order these paragraphs? _____

_____

5 List the transitions used in the essay. _____

_____

6 What function is served by the last paragraph? _____

_____

7 Which specific words in the last paragraph refer to key words

—topics or subdivisions—of the rest of the essay? _____

4 Now read the following essays. The order of the paragraphs is
jumbled. First, find the paragraph that has the thesis sentence,
announcing the general subject of the essay. Then find the
divisions of the topic. You should be able to discover the order
of the paragraphs by following the order of the subdivisions of
the topic. The final paragraph will be a summary of the main
points of the essay. You can also use transition words as clues.
After you have decided the correct order of the paragraphs,
indicate that order in the blanks to the left of each paragraph.

____ However knowledgeable a teacher may be, his teaching
will be largely ineffective unless he shows a true interest in his
job and his students; this interest is usually obvious to the student and cannot be feigned. A teacher who makes a real attempt to answer his students' questions, makes himself
available at reasonable times for consultation, and is always
prepared for his classes, creates an atmosphere for the student
that is conducive to learning the material, which is, after all,
the primary purpose of the class. The professor who merely
goes through the motions of teaching and who does not make
a genuine effort to help the student overcome his difficulties
creates a wall between himself and his students. The student,
if he is to learn, must be able to let the instructor know about
his problems. He will be reluctant to do this unless the teacher
has demonstrated a real desire to help his students.

____ An ideal teacher, then, is one who reflects a real interest
in his students and their education by keeping himself knowledgeable and up-to-date on the subject, by making his lectures
as interesting and lively as possible. He must also provide a fair
means of evaluating the progress that the student has made in
the subject. If a teacher is truly motivated to help the student,
the results should be obvious.

____ A fair evaluation of a teacher should include consider-
ations of three basic aspects of instruction. The first and most
important criterion should be an evaluation of the teacher's
motivation, that is, whether he is genuinely interested in his
students or whether he is merely interested in showing up in
order to collect a paycheck. Secondly, the instructor's knowledge of the subject should be evaluated, as well as his ability to

convey interest and enthusiasm for the material to his students. Finally, the teacher should be rated on the fairness and completeness of his tests and grading.

_____ The teacher who is properly motivated generally tries to make his instruction clear and attention-holding. Nothing is more discouraging to a student than a teacher who seems ill-at-ease with the subject matter, who is unable to work assigned problems, or who is consistently unable to answer intelligent questions on the subject. Because a thorough knowledge of the subject usually represents an interest in the course material, well-informed teachers are usually fairly interesting speakers. However, occasionally, teachers who have the most complete knowledge of a subject waste their knowledge and talents by failing to hold the students' interest. It is almost impossible for the student to develop any interest or curiosity about a subject when the teacher presents it as dull, tedious, cut-and-dried.

_____ Finally, the teacher should be able to test the student in such a way as to reflect the knowledge of the student in all phases of the material and at the same time make it possible for a student who understands the course thoroughly to make a good grade on the examination. The test should cover all topics of the test material to an extent proportional to the time spent in class on each topic. The student must be able, however, to receive a grade that accurately reflects his knowledge and preparations, or he may possibly become either discouraged or overconfident, depending on whether the exam is too hard or too easy.

5 This essay has no thesis sentence or thesis paragraph. However, look at the transition words closely, and indicate the correct order for this essay.

_____ The teacher should also show a real interest in his students. A student can tell if a teacher is interested in the subject and trying to interest the students in it or if he really doesn't care if the students listen or are interested or not. If a student feels that the teacher isn't interested, he will lose interest, too.

_____ Therefore, to evaluate a teacher, one must check his ability to explain the subject and to make a point, to check his testing and grading fairness, and to check to see if he has a real interest in his students or if he really doesn't care.

_____ But the most important criteria used in evaluating a teacher should be his ability to explain the subject clearly and to get his point across. If a teacher can't make the students understand what he is saying, he is of no use to them. The teacher should also try to explain the subject in the most interesting, relevant way possible, for if a student isn't interested in what the teacher is saying, he probably won't listen. If this happens, the student gains nothing, and the teacher is just wasting his time.

_____ One important factor used in evaluating a teacher is his testing. Does he choose fair questions emphasized in the lectures and readings, or does he test on obscure little facts designed to see who can memorize the book? Are the questions stated clearly, or is each one written in codelike language? In grading papers, is he objective and willing to admit to an error if he makes any? If his testing and grading procedures are not fair, the students will lose respect for him and stop really trying. The teacher's assigning of grades at the end of the quarter should also be fair. If the grades are curved, they should be curved in a manner such that no one benefits more than someone else.

1 What principle of organization is used to order these paragraphs? _____

_____

2 Which paragraph did you choose to be the last paragraph? What words in the paragraph influenced your decision? What clues did you use? _____

_____

_____

6 Read this thesis paragraph closely, as if it were beginning an entire essay.

Today, to get ahead in the world, one needs "pull"—knowing the right people—rather than merit. For both social acceptance and career advancement, "whom you know" is more important that "what you know."

228

1 What will the topic of the essay following this paragraph be?

_____

_____

2 What will the topics of the development paragraphs probably

be? _____

_____

3 Which development paragraph will probably be first? _____

_____

7 Now read this thesis paragraph.

    Even though many people believe that acquiring a college education will increase a person's earning power, this is not always true, but there are certainly reasons for attending college other than increased earning power. A college education improves a student by exposing him to different people and ideas, some of which may be completely new to him, and it improves a student by further broadening the education he has begun in high school.

1 Which sentence is the thesis sentence? _____

_____

2 What will be the main supporting details of the essay? _____

_____

3 Which main supporting detail will come first?_____

_____

4 What function is served by the first sentence? _____

_____

8 Read the following essay, paying close attention to the organization of the paragraphs.

229

One of the most aggravating things about owning a sheepdog is giving it a bath, especially if the dog weighs over a hundred pounds. If you are financially able, you can pay to have it done, but fifteen dollars every week can get expensive. For the past year, in order to save money and have a clean dog, I have made it my job every Saturday to wash my sheepdog.

As my dog is so big, I have to wash her in the bathtub. Also, in order to control her while she is in the tub, I have to be in there, too. I first fill the tub with warm water and put a lot of dishwashing liquid in to make the water soapy. This is done in order to let her feet soak while I am bathing her. Also, this gives me soapy water to help in washing her.

After I put my dog in the tub I will use either a bar of Ivory soap or a bottle of dog shampoo to get her clean. As she is so big and her hair is so long, a bar of soap is cheaper to use, for it usually takes a whole bottle of shampoo to get her clean. I recommend Ivory soap because if you drop it, it is easy to find because it floats.

The next step, and probably the most important, is the rinsing. Because of her long hair, it is also the hardest part of the bathing procedure. For this step I recommend a spray hose similar to the one on the kitchen sink. You can buy these hoses in different lengths, and they are made so that you can attach them to the shower head or the tub faucet. I always spend more time rinsing my dog than washing her, because as the soap dries on her, she will scratch constantly.

When I have finished rinsing her and she has finished shaking the excess water off, I attempt to dry her with a towel. This is really a wasted step, but I do it anyway. I occasionally try drying her with a hot comb, but I have found that a vacuum cleaner on the blowing side works better and takes less time, because of her long hair.

When I have finished washing and drying my hundred-pound long-haired dog, I feel like falling out on the living room floor with a can of cold beer. Also, I feel as if I have done a day's work.

1 Does this essay have a thesis sentence? Which is it? _____

_____

2 What principle is used to order the supporting paragraphs?

_____

230

3 What is the function of the last paragraph? _____

_____

4 Does this essay need an explanation of its subdivisions in the

thesis sentence? Why? _____

_____

5 Which specific words in the last paragraph "sum up" the rest

of the essay? _____

_____

9 Read the following essay. Underline the supporting details as
you read.

One of my favorite pastimes is cooking. I have found that a
favorite of my family and friends is Red Velvet Cake. Most
people say this particular cake is extremely hard to make, but
I have found the process to be rather easy.

Using a large mixing bowl, I add 1½ cups of sugar to 2 eggs
and hand beat them thoroughly. I sift 2 cups of flour and 1
teaspoon of soda into the bowl and again mix thoroughly. Now
I add 1 cup of buttermilk and 1½ cups of cooking oil, and again
mix thoroughly. Finally, 1 teaspoon of vanilla and 2 ounces of
red food coloring are added, in that order. After beating two
minutes with an electric beater, I pour the mixture evenly in
four well-greased 10-inch cake pans. The cake pans are placed
uniformly in the oven at 350° and baked for 30 minutes or until,
when touched lightly on the surface, the cake springs back.

For the icing, again using a large mixing bowl, I add one box
of powdered sugar to 8 ounces of cream cheese, and I let this
mixture sit at room temperature until the cream cheese
becomes fairly soft. When the cheese is soft, I cream the ingredients together until a slightly thick texture is reached and
then set it aside until the cake is ready.

I take the cake from the oven (if test or time indicates it is
done). Starting with the biggest of the four layers, I place it on
a cake plate and ice it with the now smooth filling, then sprinkle with pecans or any other nuts. Using this same process, I ice
and sprinkle the remaining three layers, using more for the top
layer than any other to give the cake a fancier look.

While the cake cools, I begin now with a glass of milk to enjoy a delightfully different flavor.

1 What is the topic of this essay? _____

2 Which is the thesis sentence? _____

3 List the major supporting ideas. _____

_____

4 What transitions are used to introduce the topic of each paragraph? _____

_____

5 What is the order of arrangement used in this essay? _____

_____

6 What is the function of the final paragraph? _____

_____

7 Which specific word is a summary word? _____

10 Read the following essay. Underline the transitions as you read.

In this paper I plan to give you some of the details for putting in a CB radio in about twenty minutes, in two easy steps.

First of all, you take the radio out of the box and put it off to the side. If you want to mount it under the dash, you will need a drill. Take the bracket, and place it exactly where you want it. With a pencil, draw out the holes in the bracket on the spot where you want the radio. Set the bracket down, and take the drill in your hand. Drill through the circles you have drawn. Then take the bracket, and bolt it where you have drilled the holes. Then take the CB radio and fasten it in the bracket. Now you have mounted it, and you are ready for wiring it up.

In wiring up the CB, you look for two wires. The wires should be red and black. The red wire is the hot or power wire, and the black is the ground wire. One of the best places to place the hot wire is in the fuse box; so take a knife and pry out one end of the metal part of the fuse and clamp the fuse back down. Next find a screw that is connected to metal, and unscrew it just a little. Place the ground wire around the screw, and tighten it down.

Now you have successfully put in and wired up your CB radio, but you should not turn the radio on until an antenna is installed. Because the antennas and sets have different directions for each model, you should either consult your manual or have a professional install the antenna. But at least, the two simple installation steps above will save you money and time.

1 Which sentence is the thesis sentence? _____

_____

2 What are the two major supporting details developed in the

essay? _____

_____

3 What transition introduces the first of these details? _____

4 List the details used to develop and illustrate this first step.

_____

5 List the transitions used in this paragraph. _____

_____

6 What principle of arrangement is used in this paragraph?

_____

7 What transition introduces the second major group of detail?

_____

8 List the details used to develop and illustrate the second step.

_____

_____

9 List the transitions used in this paragraph._____

_____

10 What principle of arrangement is used in this paragraph?

_____

11 What principle also is used to determine the order of the para-

graphs in relation to each other? _____

12 What is the function of the last paragraph? _____

_____

13 What specific words in the last paragraph let the reader know

it is a summary paragraph?_____

How would you expect these thesis sentences to be developed
in an essay?

11 When I'm bored and feeling listless, I watch television, listen
to the radio, or play cards with my friends.

_____

_____

_____

_____

12 It makes good sense to drive small cars for two major reasons.

_____

_____

_____

_____

13 Adjusting the valves on a Volkswagen is easy, but three simple
rules must be followed as closely as possible.

_____

_____

_____

_____

Writing Assignment

4 Now, choose one of these sample thesis sentences, and develop it into an essay.

a. No matter what sort of school you attend, there are two types of students who are always around.
b. There are two kinds of teachers.
c. Though I realize this is an unpopular opinion, I prefer to live in a small town (or in a large city or in the country).

_____

_____

_____

_____

_____

_____

_____

_____

_____

_____

_____

_____

_____

_____

_____

_____

_____

_____

_____

_____

Readings_____

Does Sleep Help You Study?

Eric Hoddes

15 Read the following essay carefully. You may test your understanding of the essay by answering the questions on vocabulary, structure, and meaning which follow the essay.

[1] Sleep helps us remember, assuming that it *follows* study. If sleep precedes study, it can turn out to be worse than no sleep at all.

[2] The beneficial effects of sleep on memory were first studied by J. G. Jenkins and Karl M. Dallenbach in 1924. They found that individuals who slept after memorizing material recalled more than those who stayed awake. Recent experiments have confirmed this sleep effect.

[3] It doesn't seem to make much difference whether a person sleeps immediately after learning or waits a few hours. What is important is the sleep. In a study by psychologist Bruce Ekstrand and others at the University of Colorado, three groups of people learned a word task. One group immediately went to bed for seven hours. Another stayed awake for seven hours, then slept for seven hours. The third group stayed awake the full 14 hours, after which all individuals were tested for their recall. Recall was about the same for the two sleep groups, but both had better recall than the group that stayed awake.

[4] **Dreams and Sleepwalking.** The procrastinator's approach—sleep before you learn—won't help your memory at all. In fact, a short period of sleep just before new learning can seriously increase forgetting, what Ekstrand calls the "prior-sleep effect." Everyday examples of this are common: a person is awakened by the telephone in the middle of the night, talks for a while, goes back to sleep, and remembers nothing of the call the next morning. The prior-sleep effect may also explain why a person forgets dreams he had early in the night, or when he sleepwalks.

[5] It doesn't take much prior sleep to disrupt memory. In another Ekstrand experiment, subjects slept for a specified period of time, were awakened, and given a list of material to memorize. The researchers made sure the subjects were wide

236

awake before they put them through their memorizing paces. Subjects were tested four hours later for recall.

[6] Ekstrand found that prior sleep of 30 minutes, one hour, two hours, and four hours significantly impaired memory. If the students were awakened two or four hours before learning, however, their memory was no longer affected by the sleep. Also, sleeping for six hours produced less forgetting than four hours or less of prior sleep.

[7] **The Stages of Sleep.** Researchers have attempted to find out if the various stages of sleep affect memory. The Rapid Eye Movement (REM) phase is characterized by an active central nervous system, with increased heart rate and brain temperature. In the four stages of non-REM sleep, the body is relaxed, with slow and regular respiratory and circulatory functions. The stages of sleep didn't seem to matter. Usually when researchers woke up subjects in various sleep phases, they didn't find any memory difference.

[8] Hormones may be one cause of the prior-sleep effect. Researchers Elliot Weitzman, Jon Sassin, and Ismet Karacan, among others, found that sleep increases release of a hormone called somatotrophin. Hormone levels rise quickly within 30 minutes after a person falls asleep and remain high during the first half of the night. The levels subside in the latter part of the night.

[9] For the last year and a half I have studied how somatotrophin affects laboratory mice that learned to discriminate between black and white alleyways in a maze. They were injected with the hormone at various times before and after training. I then measured memory loss four weeks later. When somatotrophin was injected five minutes before training, memory was severely disrupted, but if the hormone was injected 90 minutes before training, there was no significant difference in recall.

[10] If somatotrophin operates the same way in humans, people who were awakened early in sleep may have had poor recall because of the high hormone levels in their system. These levels gradually return to normal after awakening, which may account for the disappearance of the prior-sleep effect after the subject is awake for a while.

[11] If you don't plan to go over and relearn material you study, it is best to sleep a while (four hours or longer, if possible) between the time you study and the time you have to recall the information. Don't sleep before you study unless you allow yourself a period of time of being awake before you start studying seriously. And allow for an undisturbed period of sleep.

Reading for Meaning

1   Locate the underlined words in the essay, and reread the sentences in which they appear. Write your own definition of what the word means in that sentence. Use a dictionary if necessary.

assuming _____

precedes _____

beneficial _____

recalled _____

task _____

procrastinator's _____

prior _____

effect _____

disrupt _____

subjects _____

specified _____

paces _____

significantly impaired _____

affect _____

phase _____

The words in the left-hand column are underlined in the essay. Reread the sentences in which they appear, and pick, from the choices at the right, the word that is closest in meaning. Circle your answer.

characterized	identifiable	naturalized	charred
respiratory	postponing	sweating	breathing

circulatory	blood-conveying	surrounding	periphery
functions	occupations	purposes	gatherings
discriminate	distinguish	extinguish	individual
maze	confusion	labyrinth	perplexity
injected	orbited	protruded	introduced fluid to the blood
severely	extremely	sternly	austerely
gradually	in an incline	in stages	in vectors
account	narrate	explain	transact

Reading for Structure

2 Which sentence tells the reader the central idea that this essay develops?

_____

3 What is the subject developed in paragraph 2? _____

_____

4 What is the subject developed in paragraph 3? _____

_____

5 Which sentence serves as a transition device between paragraphs 2 and 3?

_____

6 What is the subject developed in paragraph 4? _____

_____

7 Which sentence, if any, is the topic sentence in paragraph 4?

_____

8 What examples does the author use in this paragraph to illustrate the "prior-sleep effect"? _____

_____

9 The subject of paragraph 5 is a second experiment performed by Ekstrand. What transition phrase introduces the topic?

_____

10 What is the subject of paragraph 6? _____

_____

11 What is the subject developed in paragraph 7? _____

_____

12 Which sentence, if any, is the topic sentence of paragraph 7?

_____

_____

13 What is the general subject developed together by paragraphs

4 to 7? _____

_____

14 What is the general subject developed by paragraphs 2 and 3?

_____

_____

15 What is the relationship between the general ideas developed

by these two groups of paragraphs? _____

_____

16 What is the subject developed in paragraph 8? _____

_____

17 Which sentence, if any, is the topic sentence of this paragraph?

_____

_____

18 What is the subject developed in paragraph 9? _____

_____

19 Which sentence, if any, is the topic sentence of this paragraph?

_____

20 What subject is developed in paragraph 10? _____

_____

21 What transition phrase introduces this subject? _____

_____

22 What general subject is developed in paragraphs 8 to 10?

_____

23 What is the relation or connection of this general topic to the

two earlier ideas about sleep and study? _____

_____

24 Read the last paragraph again; then read the first paragraph.
Do the two paragraphs seem to say the same thing? What is the

relationship of the last paragraph to the first? _____

_____

25 What is the general organization of the essay? _____

_____

Comprehension Test

26 Is it better to sleep before or after studying? _____

_____

27   Who conducted the first experiments on the beneficial effects
     of sleep on memory? When? _____

28   What did Jenkins and Dallenbach conclude from their experi-
     ments? _____

     _____

29   Is it best to sleep immediately after studying? _____

     _____

30   What experiment did Bruce Ekstrand conduct? _____

     _____

31   What is the "procrastinator's approach"? _____

     _____

32   What is the "prior-sleep effect"? _____

     _____

33   Give an example of "prior-sleep effect." _____

     _____

34   How much "prior sleep" is required to disrupt learning?

     _____

35   Describe the Rapid Eye Movement (REM) phase of sleep.

     _____

36   How many stages of non-REM sleep are there? _____

     _____

37   Does it make any difference in which sleep phase you are
     awakened to study?

     _____

8 What is one possible cause of the "prior-sleep effect"? _____

_____

9 What hormone is released during sleep? _____

0 Describe the experiment the author conducted to examine the effect of somatotrophin on recall ability. _____

_____

_____

1 What suggestions does the author make for students? _____

_____

Writing Assignments

2 Write an essay in which you compare or contrast two methods of study that you have used recently.

_____

_____

_____

_____

_____

_____

_____

_____

_____

_____

_____

_____

_____

243

_____

_____

_____

_____

_____

_____

_____

_____

_____

_____

43 Write an essay comparing or contrasting the way you feel about attending school on Monday with the way you feel about attending school on Friday.

_____

_____

_____

_____

_____

_____

_____

_____

_____

_____

_____

_____

_____

_____

_____

_____

_____

_____

_____

_____

_____

_____

_____

44 Write an essay to describe for your instructor the methods of
cheating you have found most often used at school. Be specific
in your description, but do not use names.

_____

_____

_____

_____

_____

_____

_____

_____

_____

_____

_____

_____

_____

_____

_____

_____

_____

_____

_____

_____

_____

_____

_____

Readings_____

The Great Kissing Epidemic

Lance Morrow

Read the following essay carefully. You may test your understanding of the essay by answering the questions on vocabulary, structure, and meaning which follow the essay.

[1] There are many variations. A classic: the perfectly executed "air kiss," often performed by two women who dislike each other, who wear makeup they don't want smeared, and who both resemble Bette Davis in her middle years. They approach, incline the planes of their cheeks. Three to four inches from contact, they close their eyes in a split-second transport of fraudulent bliss, and smack their lips minutely upon nothing, as if releasing little butterflies. A somewhat rarer treat: the "hair tangle," which requires a tall, long-haired woman and a shorter man; woman inclines head to offer cheek, man goes to peck cheek, woman's hair falls in way, man ends with lips and glasses entangled in hair. Rapid disengagement follows.

[2] One chemist thinks that it all began when cavemen licked their neighbors' cheeks for the salt on them. Whatever its primal origins, social kissing seems to be resounding with greater frequency around the nation. Anyone who watched Jimmy Carter's Inaugural receptions would think that the entire capital would be down with mononucleosis by now. For a man once regarded as remote behind his barricade of teeth, Carter is a formidable social kisser, somewhat more subdued about it than Lyndon Johnson, but just as relentless. During his Inaugural parties, Carter gave a virtuoso performance, clutching women one-handed or two-handed as he delivered his kisses of greeting.

[3] Some Northerners attribute the new President's demonstrativeness to Southern ways. But an Atlanta public relations woman, Joanna Hanes, declares that "social kissing is more a Northern, sophisticated fad that seems to be moving south." In fact, like the Second Great Awakening of the 19th century, the epidemic of social kissing has persisted for some years and touched almost every section of the country. In Boston, Beacon Hill ladies can be seen rubbing cheeks at their clubs. Among usually subdued Midwesterners, the custom is growing, al-

though one partygiver in Chicago admits: "Once when I kissed a fellow on the lips, he nearly had a heart attack. He was afraid of getting germs and he wiped his mouth afterward."

[4] Perhaps nowhere is kissing more widely and elaborately practiced than in Manhattan, whose nervous system, from SoHo to Sardi's and on uptown, handles an immense traffic of social signals. But social kissing is also rampant in California, usually in the form of a double peck on the cheeks. Many believe it has gone too far. Says Los Angeles social leader Betsy Bloomingdale: "I find myself kissing and wishing I hadn't. You risk being rude if you kiss one person and not another. And there are awkward moments when you don't know whether to kiss or not to kiss. Usually, you kiss just to be safe."

[5] In one form or another, kissing has been prevalent since primitive times, but has developed mostly in the West. Among the Greeks and Romans, parents kissed their children, lovers and married persons kissed each other, and so did friends of the same or different sexes. Martial complains in one of his epigrams: "Yet, Linus, thou layest hold on all thou meetest; none can thy clutches miss: but with thy frozen mouth all Rome dost kiss." The early Christians obeyed St. Paul's injunction to "greet one another with a holy kiss" until the symbol of fellowship degenerated sometimes into sexual scandal. In the Middle Ages, knights kissed before doing battle, just as boxers touch gloves. The varieties of kisses are numerous: the kiss of treachery (Judas' example), the Mafia kiss of death, the kiss of reverence with which rabbis don their tallithim and priests their stoles. Children hold out a hurt hand for a kiss "to make it well."

[6] The French, who have had some practice, have turned kissing into a fine social art, although even they are not always sure when or how to do it. The French double kiss is routine, whether on the occasion of being accepted into the Academie Française or greeting a friend. Lately, the French have taken to kissing one another three times, alternately. Sometimes it goes on even longer. Says Regine Temam, a French librarian: "I never know when to stop now, so I just let whoever is doing it decide how long he wants to continue."

[7] Kissing or not kissing can be genetic, but not entirely so. Even the somewhat prim Swiss have begun to kiss socially. Italians are enthusiastic kissers and have been for generations; the same is true of Slavs. Arab men greet one another with kisses, as do Arab women. The British remain reticent about social kissing. The Japanese, along with many other Orientals,

regard kissing—at least in public—as a Western custom, highly unsanitary and offensive.

[8] Why is there now such an outbreak of kissing as a social gesture? According to sociologist Murray Davis, of the University of California at San Diego, "Increased kissing is part of the general inflation of intimate signals. We kiss people we used to hug, hug people we used to shake hands with, and shake hands with people we used to not to." Not to kiss or hug means one is "not relating." "Isolated individualism is out," says Davis. "Today separations are not allowed. Everyone is expected to kiss everyone else." The human-potential movement has occasionally made a travesty of E. M. Forster's "only connect!" From the hot tubs of Marin County to the baths of Esalen, the rule prevails: Whoever kisses you, you kiss back, lest you be thought to be uptight. At times, kissing carries a political message. Some feminists kiss other women on the lips in order to prove something about transcending sexuality. American men rarely kiss other men, unless they are father and son, or unless they are homosexual, in which case a public buss on the cheeks or lips is becoming more common.

[9] Social kissing takes much of its inspiration from show business, where for years an oscular promiscuity has prevailed. Kissing appeals to show people in part because it is inherently more theatrical than, say, handshaking or nodding. Kisses can be invested with any emotion from the most fervid passion to a hydrochloric malice. They *play* well. Singer Linda Ronstadt explains it in another way: "The business consists of people who are so desperately insecure and lonely, and they have to have contact; we're all affection junkies."

[10] Satirist Tom Wolfe sees a connection between show business kissing and the new campaign law. The new $1,000 limitation on contributions means, says Wolfe, that "more than ever, people in show business have a tremendous role in campaigns. Through concerts and other entertainments they can deliver a million dollars in a single evening, and in show business, this kissing has become even more rampant than it ever was. Jimmy Carter has to kiss at least 3,000 rock stars—male and female—in the next four years to pay up his debt."

[11] Many Americans get their ideas of social kissing from the television talk shows, which are orgies of lipsmacking. The rituals can be intricate. On Johnny Carson's late-night show, for example, female guests almost invariably kiss Carson; they then confront the question of whether to kiss Announcer Ed McMahon as well. Usually, they do, since McMahon has been

249

elevated over the years from the status of hired help to that of deputy executive star. But what if Doc Severinsen is sitting in?

[12] As the custom of kissing has spread from showfolk to the general population, it has raised innumerable, if minute, questions of <u>rite</u> and <u>protocol</u>. Who initiates the kiss? In a kiss between a man and woman, quite often it is the woman who makes the first move—offering her hand, inclining her cheek. But if the man is, say, the woman's boss or her husband's boss, she may wait until he leans forward into that critical distance within which the kiss occurs.

[13] If two or more couples meet simultaneously, the cross-kissing begins to resemble the start of a football game, when multiple captains of the two teams must go through all <u>permutations</u> of the handshake. Sometimes habitual nonkissers avoid kissing the hostess as they come to a party, but will have several drinks and, thus mellowed, will kiss goodnight as they leave, muttering later, "Why did I kiss that woman?" The <u>converse</u> also occurs: people kiss in a warmth of expectation as the evening begins, but then part with awkward handshakes.

[14] Timing is crucial if one is to avoid clumsy lurches and even broken teeth. Aim is vitally important. In social kissing, the lips can strike anywhere from behind the ear to the center of the mouth, depending upon the kisser's fervor or <u>sobriety</u>. Sometimes a talent for <u>evasion</u> helps. Shirley Temple Black, just retired as a U.S. diplomat, says that over the years, "I have developed a dart-and-dodge technique to avoid the kiss on the mouth."

[15] Mrs. Black has the advantage of her foreign experience. "In diplomatic circles," says she, "there is a lot of hand kissing." Men are <u>gingerly</u> with her hand, however, since she bought an Iranian ring with two stone-encrusted tigers on it. "I remember a reception in Bucharest in 1972," she relates, "when a Rumanian with a huge red beard bent over to kiss my hand. He was bent over for the longest time and when he finally made it up, there were two long red hairs in my tiger ring."

[16] Viewed with a clinical, alien's eye, kissing can seem a rather odd thing for people to do. The Chinese have even believed that it had associations with cannibalism. Kissing, of course, is not all *that* bad. But the present excesses have undoubtedly served to <u>debase</u> the currency, sometimes leaving people at a loss for ways to demonstrate degrees of affection, as well as making them unnecessarily nervous about the flu. . . .

Reading for Meaning

1 Locate the underlined words in the essay, and reread the sentences in which they appear. Write you own definition of what the word means in that sentence. Use a dictionary if necessary.

transport _____

fraudulent _____

primal origins _____

resounding _____

mononucleosis _____

formidable _____

relentless _____

virtuoso _____

demonstrativeness _____

subdued _____

elaborately _____

immense _____

rampant _____

primitive _____

epigrams _____

The words in the left-hand column are underlined in the essay. Reread the sentences in which they appear, and pick, from the choices at the right, the word that is closest in meaning. Circle your answer.

injunction	order	exclamation	judgment
degenerated	deviated	reappeared	deteriorated
treachery	betrayal	fidelity	treason

don	high title	put on	a tutor
prim	arrogant	precise	formal
reticent	reserved	silent	appalled
isolated individualism	seclusion	retirement	solitariness
travesty	mockery	journey	duty
transcending	passing through	rising above	existing with
inherently	extrinsically	within itself	gaining possession
invested	utilized	inaugurated	endowed
fervid	uproarious	burning	impassioned
rite	custom	accurateness	liturgy
protocol	etiquette	transaction	agreement
permutations	combinations	alterations	transformations
converse	associate	speak	reverse
sobriety	seriousness	lack of intoxication	affection
evasion	vagueness	avoidance	excuse
gingerly	delicate	dainty	cautious
debase	dignified	degraded	esteemed

Reading for Structure

2 What topic is developed in paragraph 1? _____

3 Which sentence in paragraph 1 is the topic sentence? _____

_____

4 Is there a thesis sentence for the entire essay, then, in paragraph 1?

_____

5 What is the topic developed in paragraph 2? _____

6 What transition is used to move the reader's attention from the phenomenon of social kissing to President Carter's kissing habits? _____

_____

7 Which is the topic sentence of paragraph 3? _____

_____

8 What details are used to illustrate the effects of social kissing in every part of the country? _____

_____

9 Paragraph 4 illustrates kissing habits in New York and California. What transition device introduces the details about New York kissing? _____

_____

10 What transition introduces the details about California kissing? _____

_____

11 What is the topic of paragraph 5? _____

12 Which is the topic sentence in paragraph 5? _____

13 How is the supporting detail in paragraph 5 arranged? _____

_____

14 What is the topic of paragraph 6? _____

15 Which is the topic sentence of paragraph 6? _____

_____

16 What transition word introduces the detail about recent French habits?

_____

17 What is the topic of paragraph 7? _____

18 Which is the topic sentence? _____

19 List the details used to illustrate the topic sentence in paragraph 7.

_____

_____

20 Considered as a group, paragraphs 2 to 7 develop one general

idea. What is it?_____

21 What is the topic developed in paragraph 8? _____

22 Is there a topic sentence in paragraph 8? _____

23 What possible cause of "social kissing" is the topic of paragraph 9?

_____

24 Which is the topic sentence of paragraph 9? _____

_____

25 What is the topic of paragraph 10? _____

26 Is there a topic sentence in paragraph 10? If so, which is it?

_____

27 What possible cause of "social kissing" is developed in paragraph 11?

_____

28 Which sentence is the topic sentence in paragraph 11? _____

_____

29 Considered as a group, paragraphs 8 to 11 develop one general

idea. What is it? _____

0 Paragraphs 12 and 13 illustrate the social problems caused by
the "kissing epidemic" for most people. What transition intro-

duces these ideas? _____

31 How does this transition move the reader from the previous
subject?

_____

32 Paragraphs 14 and 15 further develop these problems and
present one person's solution to them. How do these problems
differ slightly from the problems discussed in the previous two

paragraphs? _____

_____

33 What is the function of the final paragraph?_____

_____

_____

34 List the main ideas developed in the essay beside the paragraph groups that give details about these main ideas.

Paragraphs 2–7 _____

Paragraphs 8–11 _____

Paragraphs 12–13 _____

Paragraphs 14–15 _____

35 What, then, is the general organization arrangement of the
essay?

_____

Comprehension Test

36 Describe the two kinds of kisses discussed in the first paragraph. _____

_____

37 What is one possible origin of social kissing? _____

_____

38 According to the article, is social kissing a Northern or Southern fad?

_____

39 Why does the author mention places so far from each other (Beacon Hill, Manhattan, Los Angeles) in paragraphs 3 and 4?

_____

_____

40 What three historical facts about kissing are discussed in paragraph 5?

_____

41 Name four varieties of kisses. _____

_____

42 What is the traditional French kiss? _____

_____

43 How has the traditional French kiss changed recently? _____

_____

44 Discuss how kissing is regarded in other parts of the world besides America and France. _____

_____

_____

45 According to sociologist Murray Davis, why is there so much kissing as a social gesture lately? _____

_____

46 Why is social kissing important to show business personalities?

_____

_____

47 As the custom of kissing has spread, what are some of the problems that have arisen in social settings? _____

_____

48 What belief about kissing is still held by some Chinese?

_____

49 Does the author really consider social kissing an epidemic that is damaging? Why? _____

_____

50 How would you sum up the main idea of this essay? _____

_____

_____

_____

_____

Writing Assignments

51 Consider some social phenomena that you are familiar with—
dating, car pooling, church attendance, behavior at movies or
football games or in classes at school—and write an essay in
which you describe this behavior. Include several instances of
the behavior, and discuss any problems you think are associated with this kind of behavior.

2 Write an essay describing diets you or someone you know has tried.

_____

_____

_____

_____

_____

_____

_____

_____

_____

_____

_____

_____

_____

_____

_____

_____

_____

_____

_____

_____

_____

_____

_____

_____

Readings_____

Survival: A Primer
Michael Demarest

17 Read the following essay carefully. You may test your understanding of the essay by answering the questions on vocabulary, structure, and meaning much follow the essay.

[1] *"Hsssst!"* hissed the minked Westchester matron to a
<u>furbelowed</u> companion at New York's Grand Central Terminal.
"Come with me. I know a place that has earmuffs!"
[2] Good luck! *Bonne chance!* Happy hunting!
[3] Among other items in nationwide short supply and fierce
demand in this killing winter are woolen underwear, blankets
(wool and electric), flannel shorts, wool socks, parkas, mittens,
gloves, mufflers, ski pants, goggles, hand warmers, car batter-
ies, weather stripping, calking guns, firewood, wood-burning
stoves, electric heaters, and radios with the weather band that
tells you how frightful today is going to be.
[4] Yet another item in short supply is old-fashioned common sense. Herewith *Times*'s all-purpose, endless-winter survival guide, as composed by Senior Writer Michael Demarest:
[5] **Coddle Yourself.** Frostbite, associated in the popular
mind with <u>polar</u> explorers and Everest <u>ascenders</u>, is a real and
<u>insidious</u> danger whenever it is freezing outside. Just ten
minutes of exposure can injure ears, cheeks, tips of noses and
ungloved fingers. Smoking increases the risk, since nicotine
constricts blood vessels, hastening the cooling process. Nor
should one drink alcohol before <u>venturing</u> outside. Booze opens
up the blood vessels and <u>accelerates</u> heat loss from the body.
[6] The first symptom of frostbite is a tingling sensation in
the <u>extremities</u>. The skin turns slightly red at first and then
becomes pale grayish-yellow and numb. Pain subsides and
sometimes blisters begin to appear. At the first signs, the victim
should be brought inside and the affected parts warmed with
<u>tepid</u>, not hot water. Snow should never be massaged on a frost-
bitten area. Second- and third-degree frostbites are treated like
burns; sometimes victims are hospitalized. Thus it is only <u>com-
monsensical</u> to suit up for winter as if it were a mortal foe—
which it can be.

[7] Coddle Your Car. Cars get the blahs, just as people do in the cruelest months. The battery is the auto's tenderest part: in freezing temperatures, it loses up to 50% of its power. To keep it happy, the car should be garaged at night, with a blanket over the hood or a warming watch light hung inside. To keep the battery charged, the driver should stay in second gear for as long as possible at speeds under 50 m.p.h.; when the car is in high gear, the generator does not produce enough energy to beef up the <u>down-drawn</u> cells. Never try to start the car when any <u>accessories</u>—heater, radio, windshield wipers—are turned on. Keep an <u>aerosol</u> can of ether in the car. You may not have to use it to fight off bears or buffaloes, but it can be a useful way to whiff alive a cold, dank motor.

[8] Eat Hearty. The <u>metabolism</u> works overtime when the body is exposed to cold. As the human's heat pump, the body has to be fueled—with food. In Maine logging camps, a typical meal consists of vegetable soup, baked beans, bread and jam, macaroni and cheese, ground-beef casserole, pancakes, spaghetti and meatballs, beef stew, fresh baking-powder biscuits, in no particular order. Somewhat more delicately, Julia Child girds for winter with bean soup, enriched with leftover beef or lamb stew or whatever, and home-baked bread. And long johns.

[9] Old Asian hands swear by *kimchi,* a fiery, vile-smelling Korean dish <u>concocted</u> of Chinese cabbage, garlic, ground red pepper, scallions, onions, ginger and (it is said) a dash of dynamite. To bring the <u>mishmash</u> to the properly explosive level, one should seal it in a crock and bury it beneath the ground for several days of <u>fermenting</u>—the longer the better. After a few gulps of *kimchi,* the round-eyed <u>tyro</u> breaks into a heavy sweat and for hours thereafter exhales such a powerful <u>stench</u> that he is guaranteed front place in <u>queues</u> for buses or movies—in fact, the queues will probably dissolve entirely as soon as he appears.

[10] More practical for winter shut-ins is one of the vitamin-rich stuffed-cabbage dishes lovingly described in George Lang's *The Cuisine of Hungary.* "Housewives," he writes, "usually began preparing it on Saturday morning; toward evening, when it was ready, they wrapped it (the covered casserole) neatly in a cloth and tucked it in at the foot of someone's bed. It served as a remarkable foot-warmer throughout the winter months. . . . On Sunday it was eaten, and the leftover was tied up in the same manner and again laid in bed."

[11] Sleep Warm. Bed—with or without a cabbage casserole—is the ultimate <u>refuge</u> and <u>solace</u>. Two in bed are always warming company, and three or four or more, bundling in the name of survival, can generate more heat than Consolidated Edison. T. H. White, the chronicler of Camelot (*The Once and Future King*), took to bed all winter in his Channel Island cottage. He spread layers of newspaper over the mattress, covered them with a blanket, put on sheets, added a blanket or two, topped it off with a goose-down quilt and, spurning electric blankets, installed his red setter in the cabbage-casserole position.

[12] **Be of Good Cheer.** For Americans unused to it, a long siege of cold can be terribly depressing—particularly for those who live alone in apartments or country homes. Cabin fever sets in. The suicide rate soars. Psychiatrists are too busy to answer phones. Getting to and from school and supermarket is an ordeal. Getting to and from work is sometimes an impossibility, especially for suburbanites tied to commuter trains that seem to die in their tracks when the first snowflake falls. The house is chilly and the family short-tempered. Winter stress can be aggravated by the thought of pyramiding fuel bills and the cost of coffee and the unavailability of vegetables. It is time to turn up the thermostat of the soul.

[13] One sure cure for cabin fever is to invite friends, near neighbors, unknown potential friends—or whole families—for an evening or a night or a weekend. For example, in Wheaton, Ill., 22 neighbors of Sandy and Alan Bergerson turned down their furnaces and converged for an overnight stay in the Bergerson home, bringing with them soda, beer and potato chips and their own breakfast. The neighbors disengaged reluctantly on Sunday afternoon, hoping that it would stay cold so they could repeat the marathon in another house, another time..

[14] In any case, whatever the company, the warmth will emanate from the assembled souls, assisted by, say, mulled wine, Mozart and mozzarella. Or glögg, goulash and Gershwin. Or how about risotto, Ronstadt and Romanée-Conti?

[15] It takes a crisis to jolt Americans out of their soft, sure ways, their near-total reliance on delivered technology: gas, electricity, oil, cars, trains, buses. To rediscover self-reliance and individual responsibility, and the kind of joy that can be pressed most sweetly from hard times. To reestablish old wisdom and simple certitudes: hot chestnuts in the hand, calories in the tum. Above all, it is a time to take private inventory of friends and bosses, associates, acquaintances and lovers, past, present and putative.

Reading for Meaning

1 Locate the underlined words in the essay, and reread the sentences in which they appear. Write your own definition of what the word means in that sentence. Use a dictionary if necessary.

furbelowed _____

polar _____

ascenders _____

insidious _____

venturing _____

accelerates _____

extremities _____

tepid _____

commonsensical _____

down-drawn _____

accessories _____

aerosol _____

metabolism _____

vile-smelling _____

concocted _____

The words in the left-hand column are underlined in the essay. Reread the sentences in which they appear, and pick, from the choices at the right, the word that is closest in meaning. Circle your answer.

| mishmash | soup | mixture | concoction |
| fermenting | turbulence | agitation | reacting chemically |

tyro	beginner	gourmet	professional
stench	foul odor	aroma	fragrance
queues	seats	lines	position
refuge	shelter	hardship	waste
solace	remedy	cure	comfort
spurning	refusing	trampling	scorning
siege	long illness	blockade	adversity
converged	approached	came together	inclined
emanate	emit	omit	precede
mulled	considered	trimmed	heated
self-reliance	dependence	independence	arrogance
certitudes	remedies	ascertains	truths
putative	supposed	future	desired

Reading for Structure

2 The subject of this essay is a collection of common sense advice about surviving winter. Which sentence is the topic sentence?

_____

_____

3 What is the function of the first three paragraphs? What do they do for the reader? _____

_____

4 The fifth paragraph develops the idea that frostbite is dangerous. What is the topic developed in paragraph 6? _____

5 In paragraph 6, the first three sentences list the symptoms of frostbite. What is the arrangement of these details? _____

_____

_____

6 What subject is developed in sentences 4 to 6 in paragraph 6?

_____

_____

7 What transition device does the author use to introduce this subject?

_____

8 What is the function of sentence 7? _____

9 What subject is developed in paragraph 7? _____

_____

10 Is there a topic sentence in paragraph 7? If so, which sentence

performs this function? _____

11 In paragraph 8, what two examples are used to illustrate the

correct way to eat in winter? _____

_____

12 What is the subject of paragraph 9? _____

13 What is the subject of paragraph 10? _____

14 What is the subject of paragraph 11? _____

15 Which sentence is the topic sentence in paragraph 11? _____

_____

16 What transition device is used to link the subjects of para-graphs 10 and 11?

_____

17 What topic is developed in paragraph 12? _____

18 What is the relation between this topic and the topic developed

in paragraph 13? _____

265

19 What is the function of the last paragraph? _____

_____

20 List the areas in which the author gives advice, together with the numbers of the paragraphs in which he illustrates each bit of advice.

Paragraphs 5 and 6 _____

Paragraph 7 _____

Paragraphs 8–10 _____

Paragraph 11 _____

Paragraphs 12–14 _____

21 What, then, is the general organization of the essay? _____

_____

Comprehension Test

22 Listed below are the five areas of survival that are covered in the essay. Put them in order by placing numbers by each area.

_____ Be of good cheer
_____ Coddle your car
_____ Sleep warm
_____ Coddle yourself
_____ Eat hearty

23 How long an exposure to freezing weather is necessary to get frostbite?

_____

24 Are smokers and drinkers more prone to frostbite? Why?

_____

25 What are the first symptoms of frostbite? _____

_____

266

26 Is snow a good remedy for frostbite? _____

_____

27 How can you help protect and recharge your battery? _____

_____

28 What gas is useful in cranking a cold engine? _____

_____

29 Describe a typical meal at a Maine logging camp. _____

_____

30 Why do loggers eat so much? _____

_____

31 What is *kimchi?* _____

32 How does it help ward off the cold? _____

_____

33 What two functions did cabbage casserole serve in Hungary?

_____

_____ __

34 How does the author suggest staying warm in bed? _____ _

_____

35 What is cabin fever? _____

_____

36 What are some of the characteristics of cabin fever? _____

_____

37 What is one sure cure for cabin fever? Why? _____

_____

38 Do you think this article is humorous? Why? _____

_____

_____

39 Do you think this article gives some good advice for winter

weather? Give examples. _____

_____

_____

Writing Assignments

40 Write an essay, using the previous essay on winter as a model, in which you describe the methods you have found useful in surviving an extremely hot summer. Make your thesis statement a generalization about the methods of survival; then describe them each in detail.

_____

_____

_____

_____

_____

_____

_____

_____

_____

_____

_____

_____

_____

_____

_____

_____

_____

_____

_____

41   Describe, in an essay, the climate you consider ideal, and explain your reasons for preferring that sort of climate.

_____

_____

_____

_____

_____

_____

_____

_____

_____

_____

_____

_____

_____

_____

_____

_____

_____

_____

_____

_____

_____

_____

Readings_____

Do College Students Drink Too Much?

Byron H. Atkinson and A. T. Brugger

Read the following essay carefully. You may test your understanding of the essay by answering the questions on vocabulary, structure, and meaning which follow the essay.

[1] Such headlines as "Students in Car Smashup after College Drinking Party" and "Drunken Fraternity Party Brings Police" are altogether too familiar. They merely confirm the belief of many a newspaper reader that all undergraduates drink, that they drink too much, and that little good comes of their drinking. In private, most college officials will readily admit that drinking is a problem on the American campus, except perhaps at such schools as Brigham Young University and Bob Jones University. For the public, the doings and undoings of the college drinker seem to hold a special fascination.

[2] If the press alone has not created the stereotype of the hard-drinking undergraduate, it has certainly accepted it. College pranks and misadventures are generally attributed to excessive drink; and when little harm is done, the incident becomes a bit of buffoonery. Some of the most popular writers of our time have created an enduring illusion of college revelry. F. Scott Fitzgerald's preoccupation with drink is second only to his preoccupation with sex. Think of college and you think of flaming youth; think of flaming youth and you think of liquor and sex. Stephen Vincent Benét's sensitive portrayal of college life before the First World War is equally moist. Students in Damon Runyon's short stories are inevitably drunk, as they "shell-road" some chorus girl on the way back to New Haven. And William Faulkner's Southern college man takes his learning lightly and his drinking seriously.

[3] This picture of undergraduate insobriety has been widely accepted. It fits nicely into the folklore surrounding higher education. Every university has a drinking song, and is frequently known by it. Yale without "Whiffenpoof" and Maine without "Stein" are inconceivable. Moreover, the thought persists that college time is a time to sow one's wild oats. To learn

to hold one's liquor well is part of the fictional Americana of "growing up." Where can it be better done than at college? Yet student manners have been fashioned, not by headlines, novels, or legend, but by an age-old tradition.

[4] During the Middle Ages student drunkenness was rarely dealt with as a university offense. Toward the close of the fifteenth century, the University of Leipzig imposed penalties for throwing water out of windows at passers-by, interfering with the hangman in the execution of his duty, and other waggish enormities; yet not until much later were two students punished for causing a drunken row. At that, punishment was quite mild. Even grave offenses were genially expiated by sconcing—treating the members of the college to a drink or so. For entertaining a suspect woman in his quarters at the Sorbonne, a clark was fittingly fined a "bachelor" of wine. And four gallons of the very best wine were required of a student who cruelly beat a servant—not for the abused domestic, but for the criminal's hale companions. Sconcing continued at English universities well into the present century, and the "beer bust" preserves the tradition, in a pale copy, on the American campus today.

[5] For that matter, any college event was occasion enough for revelry. Freshman were put through a rousing initiation which involved bullying and feasting on "better than ordinary" wine at the newcomer's expense. The custom survived at the University of St. Andrews up to the end of the nineteenth century; but the thrifty Scots were content to stand treat with raisins. Better than ordinary raisins, perhaps. American fraternities have not yet entirely broken away from this pattern of harsh initiation or from the habit of occasionally introducing liquor into the ceremonies.

[6] University guilds once observed the close of the academic year by disposing of surplus revenues in prodigious drinking bouts. On feast days, the convivial Masters of Paris promptly spent their stipends at a neighboring tavern after church services. Not many such festive occasions got altogether out of hand, but on the feast day of St. Scholastica in 1354 a bloody town-and-gown brawl broke out at Oxford. The keeper of an inn called Swyndlestock abused some students with "stubborn and saucy language," and before things came to an end sixty-three students had been killed, the town and the University had been pillaged, and the Chancellor—more brave than wise—had been fired at when he attempted to quell the tumult. Completely amicable relations between the University and the city were, in due time, restored on St. Scholastica Day,

1955, when the mayor of Oxford, a Cambridge man, received an honorary doctorate, and the vice-chancellor of the University was given honorary freedom of the city. Cambridge is, even now, thoroughly prepared for any such event, "the only duty of its High Steward being to attend the hanging of any undergraduate."

[7] The parallel between this kind of riot and the contemporary forms of student mass disturbance is apparent. The huge "panty-raid" two years ago at Berkeley, the bloody "Trolley March" at Brown in the twenties, the "gang-war" between Occidental and Pomona students in the thirties—these, with dozens of others, are somewhat subdued copies of the medieval student brawl. There is one important difference. Liquor and drunkenness, usually prime causes of such behavior five hundred years ago, play a very small part in the present-day version.

[8] Tender stomachs and heavy heads usually signaled the end of examinations in the great European universities. Not only after but before an examination and, indeed, during its progress did the knowing student cater to the thirst of his masters. The custom persisted at Oxford up to the close of the eighteenth century. It was considered good management for candidates to entertain their masters handsomely, "which they commonly do the night before examination, and sometimes keep them till morning, and so adjourn, Cheek by Joul, from their drinking room to the school, where they are to be examined ... "

[9] We find no American equivalent for this. Indeed, nothing in American college drinking, whether traditional or contemporary, quite matches the European pattern. Yet, toward the middle of the seventeenth century, about fifty students then attending staid Harvard managed to consume two hundred and seventy barrels of beer in one year. A goodly number paid their tuition in malt. And President Dunster contended with the "undoing pressures of monopolies" in his sprightly defense of Vashti Barda, who kept a tavern nearby, though, to be sure, the good woman had previously agreed not to serve students with more than a quart of beer at a time.

[10] Apparently the piety of the nineteenth century did not diminish the bibulous propensities of the undergraduate: Yale Sophomores had their rum flips, Quaker students at Haverford smuggled sherry into their quarters, and clandestine liquor parties were held in the dormitories of Delaware. The flavor of the time is perhaps best captured in the diary of William Hammond, a student at Amherst. With a number of companions he

turned a temperance lecture into a "jolly row"; and when a close friend was about to be expelled for going on a spree, Hammond, who sounds remarkably like a member of the Class of 1960, peevishly observed that "here as everywhere else, men are punished, not for sinning, but for being found out."

[11] The spirited South had rigid rules and stout thirsts. Virginia enjoyed a legendary reputation for probity and alcohol; Georgia students, the worse for liquor, broke up temperance meetings on more than one occasion; and at North Carolina a number of undergraduates got roaring drunk and rode horses through the dormitory. Even today, in our fine Southern universities, the tradition of "learning to drink like a gentleman" persists.

[12] But drinking was not confined to any one part of the nation. It vexed many a faculty and college president; and it was uppermost in the minds of a large—and influential—part of the public. Drinking and college have become a natural association. But is this association accurate portraiture or caricature?

[13] Obviously, a stereotype has developed from all of this and, just as obviously, no generalization which attempts to embrace all geographical areas, types of schools, sex differences, and classes of society can be accurate. Straus and Bacon, among others, have pointed up these differences. They found the highest statistical incidence of drinking among men in private, nonsectarian, men's colleges, and the lowest incidence among women in public, coeducational, Southern, Negro colleges.

[14] But statistics can be misleading. We were recently called by the dean of men at one of our outstanding local private colleges. "Dean," said he plaintively, "we have just had to suspend one of our men when an inspection turned up a full bottle of beer in his room. He has been advised to apply at your school. I do hope you will accept him because he is a fine boy and when his period of suspension has expired, we will want to have him back." We suspect that this institution's policy on drinking is based more on public relations than on reality!

[15] On sectarian campuses the range of opinion and administrative policy is from total abstinence to moderation. One generalization nearly always holds true. In sectarian colleges, those campuses representing the older religions, such as the Jewish, the Catholic, and the Episcopalian, tend to seek and to follow a policy of temperance whereas the younger Protestant churches try to maintain a policy of total abstinence.

[16] We know too that family income and economic status

have an influence on drinking. Among those students whose family income was $10,000 or more (in 1951), 86 per cent of the men and 79 per cent of the women drank. The other end of the scale shows that from families with incomes of $2,500, 66 per cent of the men, and 30 per cent of the women students drank. Apparently, the higher the family income, the more likely it is that the student will drink.

[17] Geographical location, ethnic differences, degree of maturity in college, and parental drinking habits all have their places in the kaleidoscope, and all warn against the acceptance of a stereotype of the college student. Aside from this, we are sure that student drinkers display the same range of drinking habits as the adult society from which they come, and that this stereotype of *excessive* college drinking must be rejected.

[18] Different contemporary societies will produce strikingly different student drinking habits. Beer, to be sure, is the typical and traditional American student tipple. But we do not find in this country, as we do in New Zealand, "Drinking Blues" given for excellence of performance in beer-drinking, universities seriously competing to find their best qualified teams— qualified both in speed and distance! Sparkling and still wines are found served at the tables of many of our more sophisticated student societies, primarily as status symbols of an unusual occasion. Where but in France would we find the *vin ordinaire* as a common and natural beverage on the student's table morning, noon, and night, and late at night? Where but in New College, Oxford, would we find that even today a moral tutor receives a drink allowance of £20 "to help put his troubled charges at ease."

[19] The American student version of the college drinking society has suffered a dramatic decline in recent years. Such illegal organizations as Phi Phi, Kappa Beta Phi (Phi Beta Kappa reversed), Theta Nu Epsilon, formed primarily for group drinking, once had widespread undergraduate popularity. Today they have disappeared from most campuses, and where they do exist they command only a slim following. In our student society, as in our adult society, drinking, when not an abuse, is a social custom. Thus our students' drinking habits are shaped by family background, religious taboos, and contemporary local standards. All too often, however, these local standards are dual in nature, and this is especially true in college or university towns. In her analysis of the Porterfield Study at Texas Christian University, Mabel A. Elliott has pointed out that college men are less likely to be formally charged by the authorities than are non-college men in the same area. The

attitude often seems to be that behavior which is criminal in the non-college adult is simply a prank when performed by the college student. Courts of law are similarly sympathetic. But this indulgent attitude is scarcely shared by the prospective employer. Paradoxically, he may have chuckled when reading about the antics of a soused collegian, but he will not hire the man.

[20] What do students themselves think about their drinking habits? Our experience is that the undergraduate of the fifties seems not to share the callow admiration of the undergraduate of the twenties for the "interesting drinker." The pale, Byronic drunk, almost an obsession among the young post-bellum literati of the twenties, finds no counterpart in the modern college or university setting. American college students do not count themselves among the "beat generation" or the "angry young men," although they may follow these phenomena with amused interest. The total abstainer, even on a "moderation" campus, is usually respected for his opinions. At an earlier time he might have been an object of ridicule.

[21] This change of attitude may stem from the fact that the drinking habits of modern students do not seem to be based upon psychological insecurity, either real or fancied. While the "lost generation" of students drank and wallowed in self-pity, our modern undergraduate, if worried or insecure, seems much more apt to seek group security through an evangelical movement or psychotherapy. When he drinks, it is usually not for surcease, nor under group pressures, but for the same reasons his adult counterpart does—conviviality, relaxation, and removal of inhibition. If he has an ideal in drinking habits, it is not the heavy drinker, the "interesting" drinker, or the drinker who creates problems for himself or his group by his drinking. It is rather the ideal of sophisticated maturity in drinking which he admires—the man who discourses easily on the "right" drinks at the "right" time, and who uses alcohol as a social ladder and not as a padded club. The "party drunk" may be tolerated and cared for after a night of fraternity-party drinking, but he is not admired or respected.

[22] We find evidence, also, of a double standard in sex roles at student parties where drinking takes place. Again, the parallel with an adult society is striking. The female role is often watchful, conservative, analytical, and "Where are the keys? I'll drive home." The male role requires no explanation to the male reader. The double standard may result from a widespread belief among students that drinking is often associated with morally questionable sexual behavior. It is a fact, of

course, that alcohol reduces ability to control learned behavior, and it is likely that it also has a capacity to weaken sexual controls. The difference in the sex role in student drinking thus becomes more readily apparent. For the woman, an instinctive conservatism; for the man, a robust wolf-howl! Perhaps our women students should not be given too much credit for this behavior since it may be more instinctive than learned. Anthropologists have pointed out that in primitive societies only the men are allowed to indulge in drinking orgies. The woman's role is to prepare the drink, police the affair, tie up the more troublesome offenders, and in many other ways act as a restraining influence.

[23] Straus and Bacon find, however, that only in a very small percentage of cases is the fraternity or sorority house the setting for student drinking. Of men questioned in their survey, 60 per cent state that their usual place of drinking is a restaurant, tavern, or bar; only 3 per cent claim it to be a fraternity or sorority house. The fact that 2 per cent name "private club" as their usual place of drinking leads us to wonder whether the Ivy League schools were well represented!

[24] The student drunk is very often, both in literature and in life, a figure of fun. The anecdotes, jokes, and party stories about him are endless, and of course they, also, feed the stereotype. At U.C.L.A. recently, the campus police answered a frantic night telephone call from a house owner complaining hysterically of strange noises and of curious apparitions on top of a nearby fraternity house. After a cautious climb to the roof, the officers confronted an undergraduate wavering from side to side, zipped up to the neck in a sleeping bag. Vainly attempting to point an admonitory finger through the stifling folds of the bag, he announced in stentorian tones, "Get lost earthlings; us Martians have taken over!"

[25] There may be reason to suspect that the student who recently sent us this anonymous post card may also have taken a couple to buck him up:

Dear Dean:
   I have never before attended a university where there is an out-and-out effort on the part of its officers to reduce student freedom to a minimum. In addition to the enormous unnecessary conglomerations of laws, rules, and regulations, there is a stupid, scurvy ridiculous bunch of armed guards called police whose sole function seems to be to hound and prey upon students. This miserable institution also offers its students: inadequate housing, no parking, outmoded recreational facilities plus crummy Kerckhoff Hall.

The university seems to have <u>inculcated</u> a desirable attitude of straight-forwardness in this individual. One professor, a sponsor of a recent student dance held in one of our large metropolitan hotels, was confronted by a slightly glassy-eyed upperclassman. "Professor," he shouted, "let me buy you a drink. You probably can't afford one on your salary!" Although the young man had a sound grasp of economics, his tact left something to be desired.

[26] Most parents and community leaders believe firmly that college administrators, and the policies which they espouse, not only play a part in developing or hardening student attitudes toward drinking but may, in fact, mold them. There is no question that extreme differences in policy and policing exist, but do they have any real effect? The traditional problem of the administrator is that, if lenient, he will get his lumps from the community; if flexible, he will receive the same lumps from the student body, and he may also find that his policy approaches reality about as closely as do the inane hyperboles of the typical college fight song. If he follows a middle-of-the-road policy, he is sure not only to draw fire from both sides but also to be accused by everyone within sight or hearing of being a contemptible, <u>temporising</u> compromiser. The recent student riot at Cornell, which followed the merest rumor that student parties in living groups would be policed to see that there was no drinking of any kind, gives a clear indication of the attitudes of students and administrators at that institution. Reports from campuses in the same geographical area, such as Dartmouth and Princeton, indicate that the occasional wild fraternity party is a respected and continuing tradition. It seems clear that a policy of "straightforward <u>hypocrisy</u>" regarding student drinking exists there, as indeed it does in the University of California. Is this better or worse than a policy which forbids student drinking of any kind, is rigorously enforced, and inevitably results in the suspension or dismissal of those guilty of violating its regulations?

[27] Colleges and universities bear more responsibility than any other social group for the behavior of the young men and women who are on their campuses. But most of the influences which mold and motivate these young people do not come from colleges and universities. Like the public school, they provide the largest and least dangerous target. Many college officers throughout the country have developed a live-and-let-live attitude. They try to avoid problems, to strengthen student government, and, above all, to evade public notice. Their hope is that, like the chameleon, they will blend indistinguishably with the

background. They have come to know that there is no formula, and that that policy is best which works at a given place, with given students, and at a given point in time. There is, of course, much which might be done in the way of education and instruction, but, except at the Yale Institute, there is very little evidence that anything is being accomplished. Perhaps the best policy was stated some one hudred and fifty years ago, when the authorities at William and Mary ordained "that the drinking of spirituous liquors (except in that moderation which becomes a prudent and industrious student) be prohibited."

Reading for Meaning

1 Locate the underlined words in the essay, and reread the sentences in which they appear. Write your own definition of what the word means in that sentence. Use a dictionary if necessary.

buffoonery_____

insobriety_____

inconceivable_____

waggish_____

enormities_____

genially_____

expiated_____

prodigious_____

convivial_____

stipends_____

pillaged_____

quell_____

tumult_____

amicable_____

staid_____

The words in the left-hand column are underlined in the essay. Reread the sentences in which they appear, and pick, from the choices at the right, the word that is closest in meaning. Circle your answer.

sprightly	animated	brisk	buoyant
piety	climate	sympathy	reverence
bibulous propensities	eating abilities	inclination to fight	drinking abilities
clandestine	orgiastic	snobbish	secret
probity	integrity	sobriety	partying
vexed	angered	troubled	influenced
nonsectarian	unaccredited	no religious affiliation	exclusive
plaintively	sorrowfully	complainingly	irritably
abstinence	abuse	denial	freedom of choice
kaleidoscope	pattern	total picture	stereotype
indulgent	humorous	lenient	gratifying
callow	immature	insensitive	shocking
surcease	escape	delay	refrain
inhibition	fear	sobriety	conditioning
apparitions	lights	imagined figures	objects
admonitory	punishing	reproaching	approving
stentorian	religious	scholarly	extremely loud
inculcated	instilled	removed	forced
temporising	inappropriate	evasive	abstaining
hypocrisy	pretense	medical	first aid

280

Reading for Structure

2 What is the central idea of this essay?_____

3 Is there a thesis sentence? If so, which is it?_____

4 What topics are developed in paragraphs 1 and 2?_____

_____

5 Which is the topic sentence in paragraph 2?_____

6 What is the topic of paragraph 3?_____

7 Which is the topic sentence in paragraph 3?_____

8 Considered as a group, paragraphs 4, 5, and 6 develop one main idea. What is that idea?_____

9 Which sentence in paragraph 3 introduces this topic?_____

10 Is the detail in paragraphs 4 to 6 arranged in chronological order?_____

11 What phrase in paragraph 7 signals the relationship between its subject and the subjects of paragraphs 4 to 6?_____

12 What is the relationship between the topics of paragraphs 8 and 9?_____

_____

13 What is the topic developed in paragraph 10?_____

14 What is the topic developed in paragraph 11?_____

15 What is the general subject developed in paragraphs 13, 14, and 15?_____

16 What is the general subject developed in paragraphs 16, 17, and 18?_____

_____

17 What topic is developed in paragraph 19?_____

_____

18 Which sentence in paragraph 19 is the topic sentence?_____

_____

19 What is the topic of paragraph 20?_____

20 Is there a topic sentence in paragraph 20?_____

21 Is there a transition to link paragraphs 19 and 20?_____

22 What is the topic of paragraph 21?_____

23 Which is the topic sentence in paragraph 21?_____

24 What is the topic of paragraph 22?_____

25 Which is the topic sentence in paragraph 22?_____

26 What transition word links the topics of paragraphs 21 and 22?

_____

27 What is the arrangement of detail used in paragraph 22?

_____

28 What is the topic of paragraph 23?_____

29 What is the general subject developed in paragraphs 24 and 25?

_____

30 What is the topic of paragraph 26?_____

31 What is the function of paragraph 27?_____

32 What are the main ideas developed in the essay? List them in order._____

_____

_____

_____

33 What, then, is the general arrangement of the detail in this essay?_____

Comprehension Test

34 What effect do the news media have on popular opinion about college students?_____

_____

35 In what ways has drinking been incorporated into the tradition of higher learning?_____

_____

36 Cite examples from the essay that show that drinking has long been a university tradition in Europe._____

_____

37 What is the major difference between today's student disruptions and those of the fourteenth century?_____

_____

_____

_____

_____

_____

_____

283

38 Describe the traditional examination preparations in European universities in the past._____

_____

_____

39 Cite examples from the essay that show that drinking has long been a university tradition in America._____

_____

_____

40 What were the results of the tests conducted by Straus and Bacon concerning college drinking?_____

_____

41 What is the normal policy of sectarian colleges toward drinking? Which group is more conservative?_____

_____

42 What influence do family income and economic status have on student drinking?_____

_____

43 List four factors (other than family income and economic status) that apparently influence student drinking.

_____

_____

_____

_____

_____

_____

44 What is the typical attitude of the courts toward college drinking?

_____

_____

45 What is the typical attitude of prospective employers toward college drinking?_____

_____

46 How do contemporary students feel about their drinking habits?_____

_____

_____

47 Why is the heavy drinker no longer admired on college campuses?_____

_____

_____

48 What explanation does the essay offer for the double standard in sex roles at student parties where drinking takes place?

_____

_____

49 Where did Straus and Bacon discover that most students drink? What percentage of student drinking occurred in fraternity or sorority houses?

_____

_____

50 What part do parents and community leaders believe the college administration plays in student attitudes toward drinking?

_____

_____

51 What problems does the college administrator have in making policies regarding drinking?_____

52 What does the author mean by a policy of "straightforward hypocrisy"?

53 How have most college administrators finally dealt with the problem of making policies governing drinking?

54 How did the authorities of William and Mary deal with the problem of drinking?_____

55 How does the author feel about the problem of student drinking? Explain.

56 What effect does the last sentence of the essay have on the reader? Why?

286

Writing Assignments

57 Write an essay in which you describe your attitudes and those
of your friends toward drinking.

_____

_____

_____

_____

_____

_____

_____

_____

_____

_____

_____

_____

_____

_____

_____

_____

_____

_____

_____

58 Write an essay comparing or contrasting the pressures you face
with the pressures faced by an earlier generation of students or
with the pressures faced by your parents' generation.

_____

_____

_____

_____

_____

_____

_____

_____

_____

_____

_____

_____

_____

_____

_____

_____

_____

_____

_____

_____

_____

_____

_____

_____

_____